ISBN: 0-9826608-3-9
ISBN 13: 978-0-982-6608-3-6

You can visit us online at: ***www.JacKrisPublishing.com***

Printed in the United States of America.

Ver. 1.0.0-2

Preface

We have designed this thorough program to be user friendly for both teacher and student. This program is arranged in **36 weekly lessons**. Each lesson consists of five exercises labeled **Day 1** through **Day 5**.

Level 2

Table of Contents

Winning
With
Writing

Level 2

Sentences

Date: _______________________

Writing is the way we communicate with each other by using words that can be read. Words are strung together to form **sentences**. In order for a group of words to be considered a sentence instead of just a group of words, it must represent a **complete thought** about someone or something.

Two parts must exist in order for a group of words to form a complete thought, a **subject** (naming part) and a **predicate** (telling part).

The **subject** of a sentence tells **who** or **what** the sentence is about. The **predicate** of a sentence tells **what the subject is** or **what the subject does**.

Does the following group of words represent a **sentence**?

Mother | cooked.

↑   ↑

Subject   **Predicate**

Yes, this is a **complete sentence** because it has a **subject** and a **predicate**, and it forms a complete thought. The **subject** tells that the sentence is about **Mother**. The **predicate** tells that **Mother cooked**.

A. Read the following groups of words and write an **X** next to each group of
    words that is a **sentence**.

1.____ The dog.

2. ____ Cindy jumped.

3. ____ The cook.

4. ____ Walked there.

5. ____ The man sang.

6.____ That dog.

7. ____ Ran backward.

8. ____ She skipped.

9. ____ We walked there.

10. ____ The dog barked.

Sentences

Date: _______________

In our last exercise (Day 1), we learned that in order for a group of words to be a sentence, it must have both a **subject** and a **predicate**. If a group of words does not have both a subject **and** a predicate, we call it a **fragment**.

Look at these examples. Is this group of words a sentence?

My sister.
↑
Subject

No, this is not a sentence because it does not have a **predicate**. A predicate would tell something about <u>who</u> **sister** is or <u>what</u> **sister** does. The above example is a **fragment**.

My sister jogged home.
↑   ↑
Subject Predicate

You can see that this group of words is now a sentence because it has a subject **and** a predicate and it forms a complete thought. The predicate **jogged** tells what **sister** does.

Let's look at another example. Is this group of words a sentence?

Jogged home.
↑
Predicate

No, this is not a sentence because there is no **subject**. A **subject** would tell <u>who</u> or <u>what</u> **jogged** home. The above example is a **fragment**.

My sister jogged home.
↑   ↑
Subject Predicate

You can see how this group of words is a **sentence** because it has a **subject** and a **predicate** and it forms a complete thought.

Sentences

Date: _______________________

A. Read the following groups of words below. Write an **<u>F</u>** on the line if the group of words is a **fragment**. Write an **<u>S</u>** if it is a **sentence**.

1.______ The puddle.

2.______ Randy jumped.

3.______ The doctor.

4.______ His lawnmower.

5.______ Grass grew.

6.______ The lady called.

7.______ Her dad arrived.

Sentences

Date: ________________________

A. Read the following sentences. Identify each underlined part as the **subject** or the **predicate**. Write **S** for **subject** or **P** for **predicate** on the lines.

1. ______ He <u>danced</u>.

2. ______ <u>Gene</u> jumped.

3. ______ The boy <u>fell</u>.

4. ______ Harry <u>slept</u>.

5. ______ The <u>box</u> opened.

6. ______ We <u>played</u>.

7. ______ <u>Flowers</u> grew.

Sentences

A. Look at the pictures below. Finish each sentence with a word from the box.
Do not use any word more than once.

burns	spins
jumps	flies
runs	bakes

1.

Tommy _________________________________.

2.

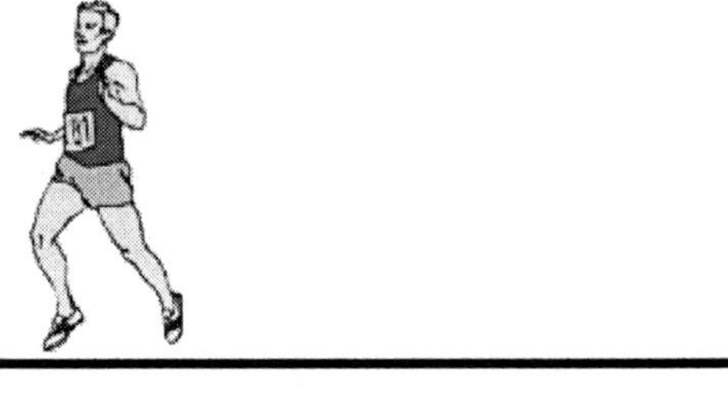

Dan _________________________________.

3.

The bird _________________________________.

4.

____

The chef _______________________________________ .

5.

____

The top _______________________________________ .

6.

____

The candle _______________________________________ .

Date: ___________________

Making Sentences More Interesting

So far we have learned to make sentences by forming complete thoughts. We form complete thoughts by making sure that every sentence has a **subject** and a **predicate**.

In the last lesson we used sentences that were very short and simple. In this lesson we will make our sentences a bit more interesting by adding words that tell **when**, **where**, or **how** something happened.

The flowers bloomed.

The above sentence tells that the flowers bloomed. It does not tell **where** they bloomed, **when** they bloomed, or **how** they bloomed.

The following sentences are similar to the last one, but they give a bit more information.

The flowers bloomed **<u>here</u>**.

The flowers bloomed **<u>yesterday</u>**.

The flowers bloomed **<u>slowly</u>**.

Do you see how these sentences add a little more information? The first sentence tells **where** the flowers bloomed. The second sentence tells **when** they bloomed. The last sentence tells **how** they bloomed.

A. Underline the words in each sentence that tell **when**, **where**, or **how**. The words in parentheses tell how the word is used.

1. Bears growl always. (when)

2. Cars stopped suddenly. (how)

3. He lifted quickly. (how)

4. We paint yearly. (when)

5. Dad mows weekly. (when)

6. Mom votes here. (where)

7. Ben jogs regularly. (when)

8. He paints skillfully. (how)

9. Snow ends abruptly. (how)

10. She danced cheerfully. (how)

**Lesson 2
Day 2**

Making Sentences More Interesting

A. **Underline** the words in each sentence that tell **where**, **when**, or **how**.

1. The cat purrs now.

2. Bob climbed carefully.

3. She rode yesterday.

4. We drove there.

5. Tracy walked slowly.

6. Ben slept nightly.

7. Jill leaped here.

8. We ran fast.

9. Sandy moved quietly.

10. It rained today.

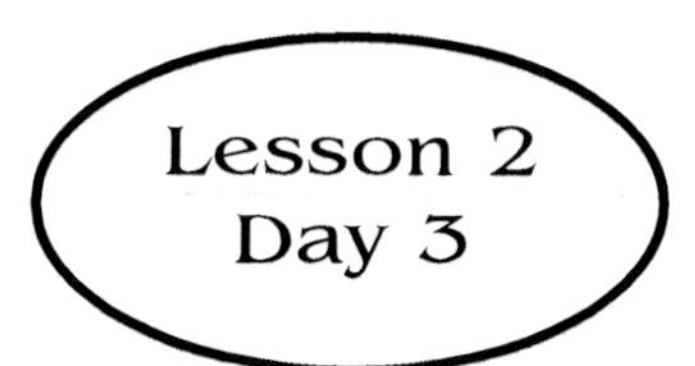

Making Sentences More Interesting

A. On Day 2, you underlined the words in these sentences that tell **where**, **when**, or **how**. In this exercise you will circle the type of information each word in bold provided.

1. The cat purrs **now**.   (when, where, how)

2. Bob climbed **carefully**.   (when, where, how)

3. She rode **yesterday**.   (when, where, how)

4. We drove **there**.   (when, where, how)

5. Tracy walked **slowly**.   (when, where, how)

6. Ben slept **nightly**.   (when, where, how)

7. Jill leaped **here**.   (when, where, how)

8. We ran **fast**.   (when, where, how)

9. Sandy moved **quietly**.   (when, where, how)

10. It rained **today**.   (when, where, how)

Date: _______________

Making Sentences More Interesting

A. Each sentence below is missing a word that tells **when**, **where**, or **how**. Choose a word to complete each sentence. Write the word on the line.

| gracefully | quickly | far | quietly | loudly |

1. The pizza disappeared ________. 

____

2. They danced __________.

____

3. He cheered __________.

____

4. The tiger jumped __________.

____

5. She read __________.

____

Date: ______________________

Making Sentences More Interesting

A. Read the sentences below and add two words of your own on the lines that tell **where**, **when**, or **how**.

1. The bunny ran ________.

   a._______________________________________

   b._______________________________________

2. They ate __________.

   a._______________________________________

   b._______________________________________

3. He walked __________.

   a._______________________________________

   b._______________________________________

Date: ___________________

Fixing Run-on Sentences

Even though longer sentences are often interesting to read, they are sometimes too long and tend to confuse the reader. Some of these sentences are called **run-on sentences**.

A **run-on sentence** is actually two sentences (each with its own complete thought) that have mistakenly been written as **one** sentence without correct punctuation to separate or join them.

One way to fix a **run-on sentence** is to **separate** it into two shorter sentences.

Here is an example of a **run-on sentence**.

Paul likes to eat he will make dinner tomorrow.

This example can be corrected by separating it into two sentences.

Paul likes to eat. He will make dinner tomorrow.

A. Separate the following **run-on sentences** into two sentences. Draw a line through the sentence where you think it needs to be separated. The first one has been done for you.

1. David studied for his test today | he will relax tomorrow.

2. Karen sang the song by herself she also sang with a group.

3. Dave takes naps he looks well rested.

4. Dad read the newspaper earlier he will watch a movie tonight.

5. Her ring was fancy she wore it every day.

6. Mom likes her new car she cannot wait to drive it.

7. The chair was comfortable Mike wanted to sit in it.

8. The sun was hot he wanted to stay inside.

9. We like to leave early today we left late.

10. I like watching movies they make me happy.

Date: ______________________

Fixing Run-on Sentences

A. Separate the following run-on sentences into two sentences. Rewrite the sentences below.

1. Mark raked the yard he mowed the grass.

2. Mom baked a cake she swept the floor.

3. The picture was torn it fell on the floor.

Lesson 3
Day 3

Fixing Run-on Sentences

Earlier in this lesson we learned that a **run-on sentence** can be corrected by separating it into two sentences.

A **run-on sentence** can also be corrected by joining the two sentences with a comma **(,)** followed by the word **and** or **but**.

Consider the following **run-on sentence**:

I help Mom wash dishes I help Dad mow.

This run-on sentence can be corrected by adding a **comma** followed by the word **and** or **but**. This is called a **compound sentence**.

I help Mom wash the dishes**, and** I help Dad mow.

A. Read each pair of sentences. Write an **X** next to the sentence from each pair that is a **run-on sentence**.

1. a. _____Bob eats his steak he eats his dessert.

   b. _____Bob eats his steak, and he eats his dessert.

2. a. _____I can go to the park I can go to the movie.

   b. _____I can go to the park, and I can go to the movie.

3. a. _____Lori and Brenda dress alike they eat the same foods.

    b. _____Lori and Brenda dress alike. They eat the same foods.

4. a. _____The flowers in the garden are red they smell good.

    b. _____The flowers in the garden are red, and they smell good.

5. a. _____My dog eats anything. He likes to wear a sweater.

    b. _____My dog eats anything he likes to wear a sweater.

6. a. _____I want a cookie, and I would like some milk.

    b. _____I want a cookie I would like some milk.

7. a. _____This pen has blue ink I have a pen with red ink.

    b. _____This pen has blue ink, but I have a pen with red ink.

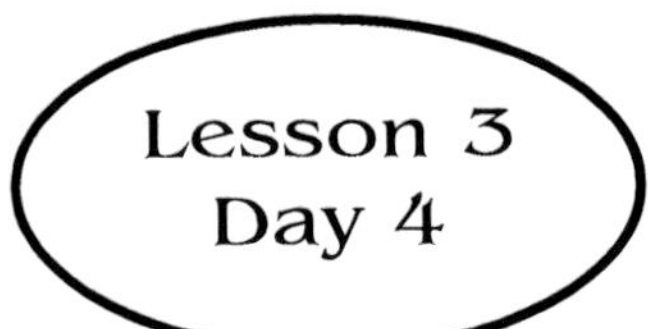

**Lesson 3
Day 4**

Fixing Run-on Sentences

A. Correct the following run-on sentences by using a **comma (,)** followed by the word **and** or **but**. Rewrite each **sentence** on the lines below.

1. My fish tank had a leak I fixed it.

2. The dog barked nobody was outside.

3. The toy was mine my sister played with it.

Date: _______________________

Fixing Run-on Sentences

A. Read the following paragraphs and underline any sentences that are **run-on sentences.**

1.   Mom and I spend time in the garden we like to pull weeds. We pick flowers from the garden. We arrange the flowers in a vase. We put them on the table. People comment on our flowers they think they look nice. This makes us feel good.

2.   I like to go to the fair they have cotton candy. They also have other fun things to do. My sister rides the merry-go-round Mom goes with her. Once I won a prize at the fair.

3.   I love when winter turns to spring. The grass starts to grow again the flowers start to bloom. I like the smell of fresh cut grass. Dad lets me drive the lawnmower. I also like summer the swimming pool will soon be open.

Correcting Wordy Sentences

In the last lesson, we learned how to correct **run-on sentences** by either separating them into two sentences, or by using a **comma** followed by the word **and** or **but**. In the last lesson a **run-on sentence** was easy to spot because it was actually two distinct sentences within one sentence.

In this lesson, the **run-on sentences** are a little harder to detect because they are not simply two distinct sentences within a single sentence.

Many times you can spot a run-on sentence when it has too many words and uses connecting words like **and** or **but**. We call these types of sentences **wordy**. In this lesson we will spot wordy sentences and correct them by using the two techniques learned in Lesson 3.

Here is an example of a wordy sentence:

> Travis likes to go fishing he likes to watch stars at night but sometimes he likes to read a good book.

You can see how there are three separate thoughts in this one sentence : 1) Travis likes to go fishing, 2) he likes to watch the stars at night, and 3) but sometimes he likes to read a good book.

Here is how you can correct this sentence:

> Travis likes to go fishing**.** He likes to watch stars at night**, but** sometimes he likes to read a good book.
>
> You can see how this **wordy** sentence was corrected by adding a **period** after the first complete thought, and adding a comma before the word **but** to separate the second and third thoughts.

A. Below are several sentences. Write an **X** next to each sentence that is a
wordy sentence.

1. ____ I do not like getting up but I do like eating breakfast I like getting
ready for the day.

2. ____ My family plays games together, and I usually win.

3. ____ I tried to climb the monkey bars but I fell today I will try to swing high
on the swing.

4. ____ I like to watch movies, but some movies are boring I do not like
those.

5. ____ My room is dirty, and I need to pick up my toys.

**Lesson 4
Day 2**

Correcting Wordy Sentences

A. Read each pair of sentences. Write an **X** next to the sentence that is a **wordy** sentence.

1. a. _____ Mom likes to make pasta but she also likes to make steak and she makes delicious green beans.

   b. _____ Mom likes to make pasta, but she also likes to make steak. She makes delicious green beans.

2. a. _____ The candy in the dish is not my favorite, but I will eat it anyway. It is sweet and chocolaty.

   b. _____ The candy in the dish is not my favorite but I will eat it anyway it is sweet and chocolaty.

3. a. _____ I liked that book it was really funny but it was too long.

   b. _____ I liked that book. It was really funny, but it was too long.

4. a. _____ The flowers in the garden are red they also smell good.

   b. _____ The flowers in the garden are red, and they also smell good.

5. a. _____ I want to go outside but my sister wants to stay inside my dad wants to go outside as well.

   b. _____ I want to go outside, but my sister wants to stay inside. My dad wants to go outside as well.

6. a. _____ The sun is so bright and the window shades are open it is too hot.

   b. _____ The sun is so bright, and the window shades are open. It is too hot.

Date: ________________________

Correcting Wordy Sentences

A. Read the following groups of sentences and underline any sentences that are wordy.

1.   I like to go somewhere warm on vacation Mom likes to go to warm places as well. I found seashells on the beach most of them were very small or broken but I kept them anyway. My big brother helped me find shells that were pretty. One shell was from a crab and one was from a snail they were interesting.

2.   My new shoes are neat. I outgrew my old shoes and Dad says he thinks I am still growing. I do like the idea of growing but I really like this pair of shoes I would like to wear them for quite a while.

3.   I like ketchup on many things it probably doesn't taste good on ice cream but I've never tried that. Mom says that I eat too much ketchup. Ketchup is good on pizza it can be kind of messy but it doesn't taste good with some toppings.

Date: ___________________

Correcting Wordy Sentences

A. Correct the wordy sentence below by using a **comma** and the word **and**.

Airplanes soar over my house I wonder where they are going.

Date: ________________________

Correcting Wordy Sentences

A. Correct the wordy sentence below by splitting it into two sentences.

Dad and I like to watch football games Mom likes to eat popcorn.

**Lesson 5
Day 1**

Correcting Choppy Sentences

We have already learned that some sentences need to be shortened because they are **run-ons** or **wordy**. Sometimes the opposite occurs and we have more than one short sentence with related thoughts right next to each other. These are called **choppy** sentences. They are difficult to read because they make the reader constantly stop and start a new sentence.

We correct choppy sentences by **combining** or **joining** them to create one longer sentence.

Here is an example of two choppy sentences:

Jimmy plays baseball. Fred plays baseball.

You can see that these two sentences are related since they both talk about **playing baseball**. Here is an example of how we could **combine** these choppy sentences into one longer sentence:

Jimmy and Fred play baseball.

Here is another example of two choppy sentences:

Jimmy plays baseball. Fred plays soccer.

Since both sentences are talking about playing a sport, we could **join** them by adding one sentence to the end of the other.   Use a word like **and** or **but** with a **comma**.

Jimmy plays baseball, but Fred plays soccer.

A. Below are several sentences. Write an **X** on the line next to those that are
   choppy sentences.

1. ____ Mike likes the rain. Bill likes the rain.

2. ____ We can make lunch, or we can make breakfast.

3. ____ Karen swims. Karen wears a cap.

4. ____ We can go to the store. We can go to a movie.

5. ____ Birds sing all day, and they rest at night.

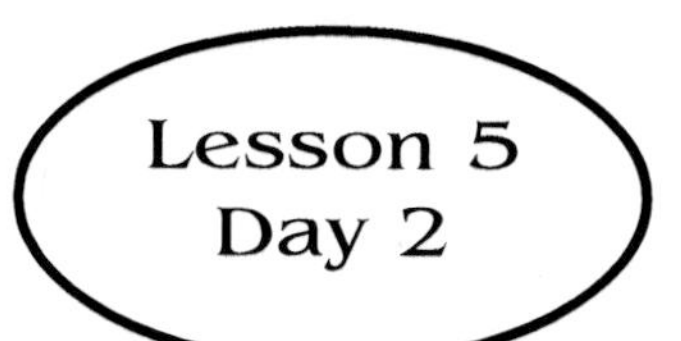

Date: ________________________

Correcting Choppy Sentences

A. On the lines next to each sentence below, write a **C** if the two choppy sentences should be **combined**, or write a **J** if they should be **joined** by using a **comma** followed by the word **and** or **but**.

1. ______ Tina walked to the house. Tina walked to the store.

2. ______ Bob likes to sleep on the couch. Bob likes to exercise.

3. ______ The den had a wooden floor. The kitchen floor had carpet.

4. ______ Brenda is a nice girl. Brenda is a caring girl.

5. ______ Gary stood near the door. Dan waited outside for his Mom.

6. ______ The show was funny. The show was long.

7. ______ Kathy stayed home. Cindy went to the post office.

Correcting Choppy Sentences

A. Combine these choppy sentences into one sentence.

1. Jim likes candy. Jim likes ice cream.

2. Greg played at the park. Ed played at the park.

3. Jill can make a pie. Jill can make a cake.

Date: _______________________

Correcting Choppy Sentences

A. Correctly rewrite the choppy sentences below. **Join** them with a **comma** and the word **and** or **but**.

Don cleaned the yard. Joe helped Dad trim the bushes.

**Lesson 5
Day 5**

Correcting Choppy Sentences

A. Correctly rewrite the choppy sentences below. You must decide if it is better to **combine** or **join** them.

I always make my bed. My sister is messy.

Date: _______________

Review of Sentences

A. Read the following sentences. Identify each underlined part as the **subject** or the **predicate**. Write <u>S</u> for **subject** or <u>P</u> for **predicate** on the lines.

1.______ The <u>bus</u> stopped.

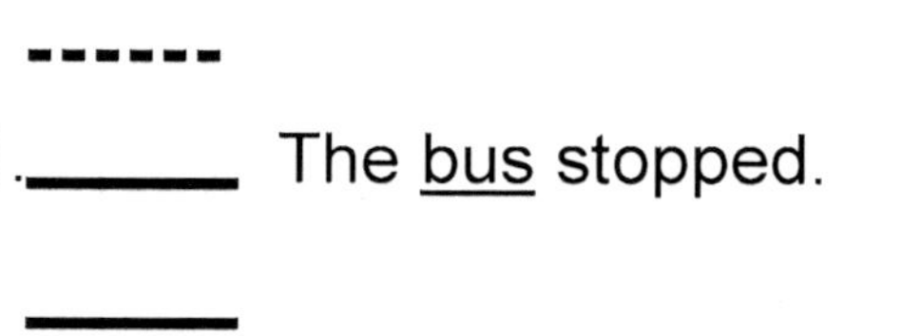

2.______ <u>Mom</u> smiled.

3.______ Bridget <u>ate</u>.

4.______ Kate <u>left</u>.

5.______ Ants <u>march</u>.

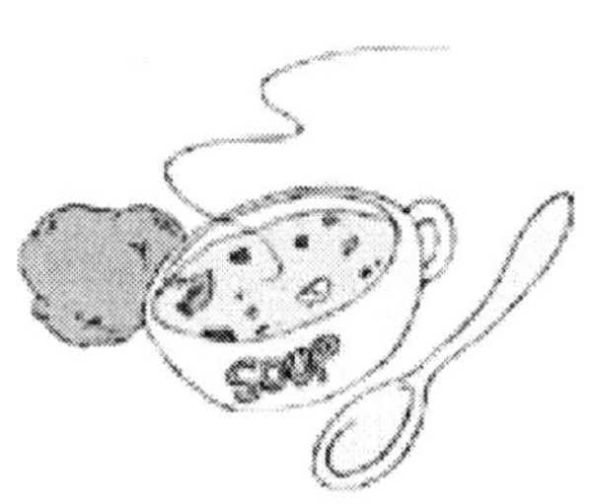

6.______ <u>Men</u> waved.

7.______ <u>Tigers</u> growl.

Lesson 6 Review Day 2

Review of Making Sentences More Interesting

A. Underline the words in each sentence that tell **where**, **when**, or **how**. The words in parentheses tell how the word is used.

1. (how) Jan stood carefully.

2. (how) Jerry walked slowly.

3. (when) We will ride tomorrow.

4. (where) The faucet leaks there.

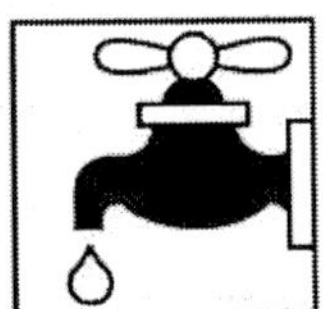

5. (how) Tracy stopped suddenly.

6. (when) She walked later.

7. (where) We live there.

8. (how) I drove slowly.

9. (when) We make a fort daily.

10. (where) The bike sat there.

Review of Fixing Run-on Sentences

A. Read each pair of sentences. Write an **X** by the sentence that is a **run-on sentence**.

1. a. _____George made a paper airplane. He used new paper.

   b. _____Barb tried on a shirt she tried on pants.

2. a. _____Our bird flew around the house he ate his food.

   b. _____My hamster exercises daily, and he plays in his cage.

3. a. _____It is raining hard I am not wearing a coat.

   b. _____Harry likes pudding. His sister likes to eat crackers.

4. a. _____You can drive the car make sure it has gas.

   b. _____Mom cooked meatloaf, and it was very tasty.

5. a. _____Mark eats four times a day Kim only eats three times.

   b. _____Sally went to the gym. Cathy did not go with her.

6. a. _____Riding in a boat is fun his boat is very fast.

   b. _____I was tired. I took a short nap.

7. a. _____This paper is interesting, but it is from yesterday.

   b. _____We got a new dog his name is Corky.

Date: _______________________

Review of Correcting Wordy Sentences

A. Read each pair of sentences. Write an **X** next to the sentence that is a **wordy sentence**.

1. a. _____Dad works on the car he paints the house and he likes to weed to the garden.

   b. _____Mom does the laundry, but she does not iron the clothes.

2. a. _____The elephant is huge, and it is very heavy.

   b. _____The turtle is slow and it is small and it has a hard shell.

3. a. _____I like reading magazines and I like reading books I do not like watching television.

   b. _____I like going out to eat, but I also like staying at home.

4. a. _____We enjoy going to the park, and we like playing with the children.

   b. _____The flowers are pink and the apple is red but the soup is brown.

5. a. _____I play in the yard, but I come in early.

   b. _____Sarah likes to play the horn and flute and she also likes to play the tambourine.

6. a. _____It is cold today, but tomorrow it will be warm.

   b. _____We wanted to go to the circus but we stopped and we ate lunch first.

Date: ________________________

Review of Choppy Sentences

A. Rewrite these **choppy sentences** below to make better sentences. Do not forget to include correct punctuation. **Combine** the first two sentences and **join** the second two sentences.

1. Bert likes to sing. Bert likes to dance. 

____

- -

____

- -

____

- -

____

2. Martha likes to clean. She does not like to cook.

____

- -

____

- -

____

- -

____

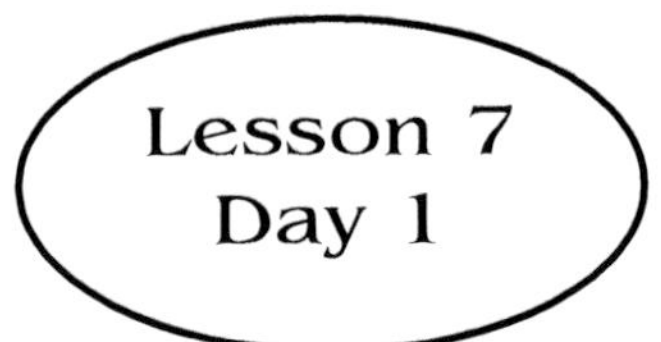

Date: ______________________

Using Strong Verbs

A **verb** is a word that shows **action**. **Action verbs** can tell **what** a person or thing is **doing**.

In Lesson 2 we learned that a sentence has to have a **subject**. The subject is a **noun** (a **person**, **place**, or **thing**) that tells what the sentence is about. The **action verb** shows action by telling **what** a noun is doing.

A **strong verb** is still an action verb, but it is **more specific** than a tired or boring verb.

Here is a sentence with the verb **played**:

Randy **played** on the trampoline.

Compare that sentence to this sentence with the strong verb below:

Randy **flipped** on the trampoline.

Of course both sentences are fine, but you can see that the second sentence is more interesting because it provides the reader with a much clearer image of what Randy is actually doing on the trampoline.

A. Read the following sentences. Underline the **boring verb** in each sentence.

1. Barry ate his meal.

2. Mom cleaned the dishes.

3. Jacob moved across home plate.

4. Claudia asked her friend.

5. I sat on the couch.

6. The truck went down the road.

Using Strong Verbs

A. Let's take another look at the sentences used in the exercise from Day 1. On Day 1, you underlined the boring verb in each sentence. Write a **strong** verb from the box below that could take the place of each boring verb in bold. Use each **strong verb** only once.

chewed	rolled	ran
questioned	scrubbed	rested

1. Barry **ate** his meal.

   ____

2. Mom **cleaned** the dishes.

   ____

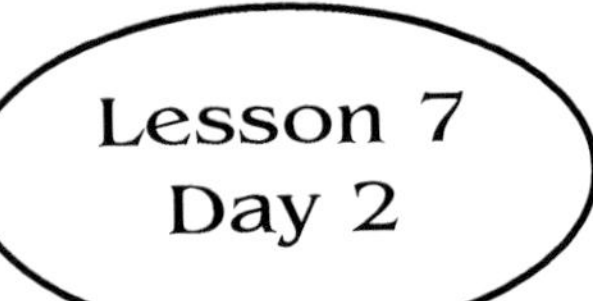

3. Jacob **moved** across home plate.

   ____

4. Claudia **asked** her friend.

   ____

5. I **sat** on the couch.

6. The truck **went** down the road.

Date: _______________________

Using Strong Verbs

A. Let's again take a look at the sentences used in the exercise from Day 2. From the box below write another **strong verb** that could take the place of the existing strong verb in bold in each sentence. Use each **strong verb** only once.

slid	relaxed	gobbled
sped	shined	quizzed

1. Barry **chewed** his meal.

   ____

   -

   ____

2. Mom **scrubbed** the dishes.

   ____

   -

   ____

3. Jacob **ran** across home plate.

   ____

   -

   ____

4. Claudia **questioned** her friend.

   ____

   -

   ____

5. I **rested** on the couch.

6. The truck **rolled** down the road.

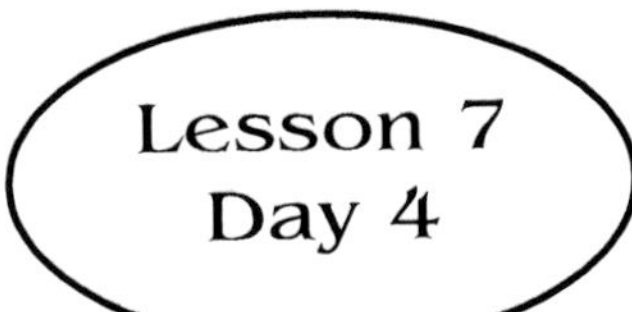

**Lesson 7
Day 4**

Using Strong Verbs

A. Write a **strong verb** from the below box to complete each sentence. Use each strong verb only once.

dripped	rose	popped
hissed	roared	bent

1. The car _____________________________ as it started.

2. The baseball _____________________________ into the air.

3. The water _____________________________ from the faucet.

4. The snake _____________________________ when it saw us.

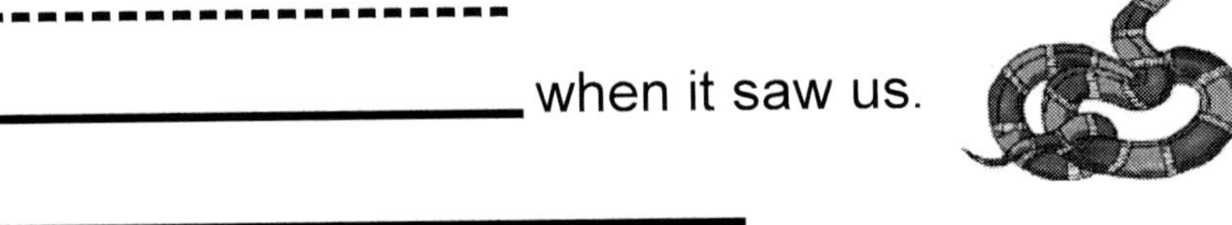

5. The golf club _____________________________ as it hit the ball.

6. The fire _____________________________ out of control.

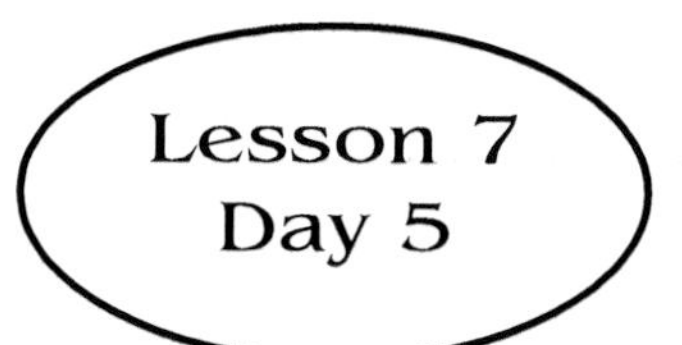

Date: _______________________

Using Strong Verbs

A. Read the following sentences. Five **boring verbs** have been underlined. Write each boring verb on the lines below. Write a strong verb next to it that could take its place in the sentence.

I play baseball every week, but sometimes I <u>sit</u> on the bench. When it is my turn, I try to <u>hit</u> the ball by <u>moving</u> the bat toward the ball. If I hit the ball it <u>rises</u> into the air, and I <u>go</u> to first base.

Boring Verbs	Strong Verbs
1. a. _________________	1. b. _________________
2. a. _________________	2. b. _________________
3. a. _________________	3. b. _________________
4. a. _________________	4. b. _________________
5. a. _________________	5. b. _________________

Date: ___________________

Describing the Action

To **describe action** in a sentence, we often use **adverbs**. Adverbs are words that tell **how**, **when**, or **where** something occurs. Adverbs are used to add more detail to sentences.

Adverbs that tell **how** something happens usually end in the letters **-ly**. The following sentence contains an adverb that tells **how**.

Grandpa walked **slowly**.

Notice that the word **walked** actually tells **what** is happening. It is a **verb**. The adverb **slowly** tells **how** Grandpa walked.

An adverb can also tell **when** or **where** something happens.

Grandpa walked **earlier**.

Grandpa walked **outside**.

As you can see, the words **earlier** and **outside** tell **when** and **where** Grandpa walked.

A. Read the following sentences. Underline the **adverb** in each sentence. The
words in parentheses will tell you how the adverbs are used.

1. (how) George rapidly lifted the gate.

2. (when) Lori ran a mile yesterday.

3. (where) The chair rocked backward.

4. (how) The clock rang loudly.

5. (where) The train moved forward.

6. (where) The boat sank there.

**Lesson 8
Day 2**

Describing the Action

A. Look at the pictures below. Underline the word under each picture that is an **adverb**.

1. jumped swiftly

3. playing now

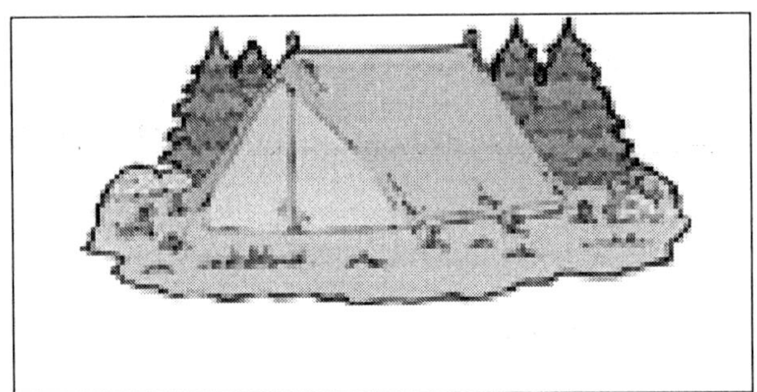

2. camped yesterday

4. performed carefully

B. Use two of the **adverbs** you underlined above to complete these sentences.

1. We moved the couch _______________________

2. The car drove _______________________

Date: ___________________

Describing the Action

A. Write the **adverb** that sounds better for each sentence.

1. **slowly**, **brightly**

____

- -

The elephant walked ___________________.

2. **loudly**, **quickly**

____

- -

Dad _______________________ wrote a letter.

3. **nicely**, **always**

____

- -

We _______________________ take our books to the library.

4. **earlier**, **loudly**

____

- -

The sun rose _______________________.

5. **above**, **below**

____

- -

The ceiling lamp swung _______________________.

6. **upstairs**, **today**

We mowed the lawn _________________________.

7. **brightly**, **outside**

The boys played _________________________.

8. **loudly**, **now**

Mom will bake cookies _________________________.

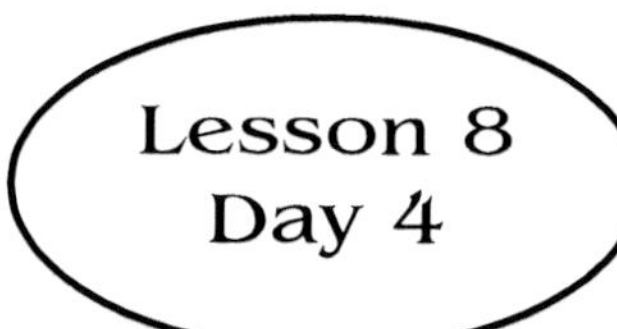

Describing the Action

Date: ___________________

A. Finish the following sentences with **adverbs** from the box below. Use each **adverb** only once.

yesterday	always	lightly
loudly	upstairs	heavily

1. Sally _________________________ rides the train.

2. Becky painted the door _________________________.

3. I read in my room _________________________.

4. It snowed _________________________.

5. It rained _________________________. It barely made the grass wet.

6. The old bus popped and backfired _________________________.

Level 2, Lesson 8 – Describing the Action

**Lesson 8
Day 5**

Describing the Action

A. Read the sentences below and use your own **adverbs** to complete them. The words in parentheses tell you what kind of adverb to use. Try to use each adverb only once.

1. The man drove ________________________. (*how*)

2. We camp ________________________. (*where*)

3. I ran ________________________. (*where*)

4. We drove home ________________________. (*when*)

5. I climb the slide ________________________. (*how*)

6. We hiked ________________________. (*where*)

7. I rode my bike ________________________. (*when*)

Date: _______________________

Using Adjectives

So far we have learned to use strong verbs and adverbs to make our sentences more interesting. To make sentences even more interesting, we can use **descriptive words** that add more detail to the **nouns** in our sentences. We call these descriptive words **adjectives**. An **adjective** tells **which one**, **what kind**, or **how many** about a person, place, or thing (a **noun**).

Here is a short and simple sentence.

Brad gave flowers.

This sentence simply makes the statement that Brad gave flowers. Could this sentence be written so that it tells the reader what kind of flowers Brad gave?

Brad gave <u>red</u> flowers.

The **adjective red** has been added which tells what color of flowers Brad gave. An **adjective** usually comes right before the noun it is describing.

A. Underline the word in each sentence that is an **adjective**. The nouns they describe are in bold.

1. The large **bear** growled.
2. The red **car** stopped.
3. Ann opened the pretty **package**.
4. The old **man** walked.
5. We ate the hot **food**.
6. Mark dove into the cold **water**.
7. The small **children** played.

B. Look at the pictures below. Write an **adjective** (descriptive word) and a
noun (naming word) for each picture. Use the words in the boxes below.

<u>Adjectives</u>

| small | pretty | muddy |
| fast | tall | loud |

<u>Nouns</u>

| music | flowers | car |
| man | ant | pig |

1.

2.

3.

4.

5.

6.

Using Adjectives

A. Look at the pictures and the words in the box below. Write adjectives from
the box on the lines below to describe each picture.

| loud   bent   light   wet |

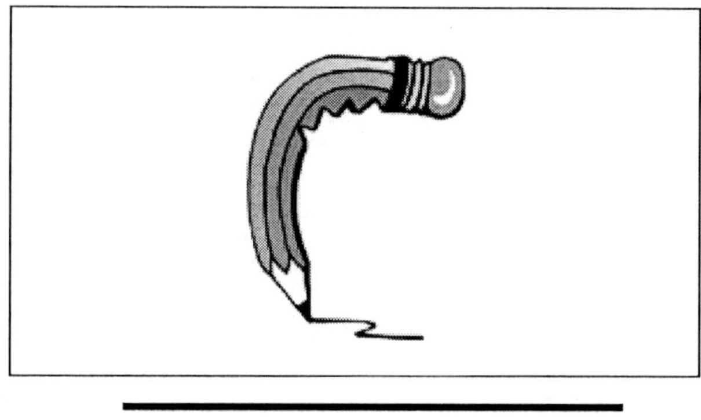

1._______________________

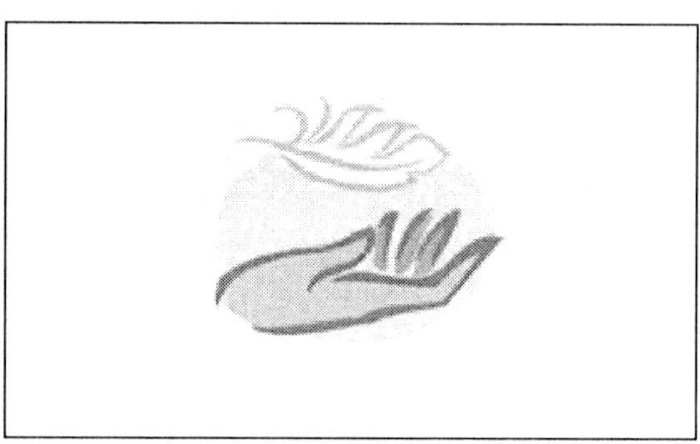

3._______________________

2._______________________

4._______________________

Date: _______________

Using Adjectives

A. Write the **adjectives** from the box below to complete each sentence.

Adjectives

| soft   green   blue   small   hard   huge   hot |

1. The _________________ baby cried.

2. There was a _________________ wave in the ocean.

3. He ate _________________ food from the oven.

4. The _________________ beans were tasty.

5. The _________________ sidewalk hurt when I fell.

6. The _________________ sky was pretty.

7. She sat in the _________________ chair.

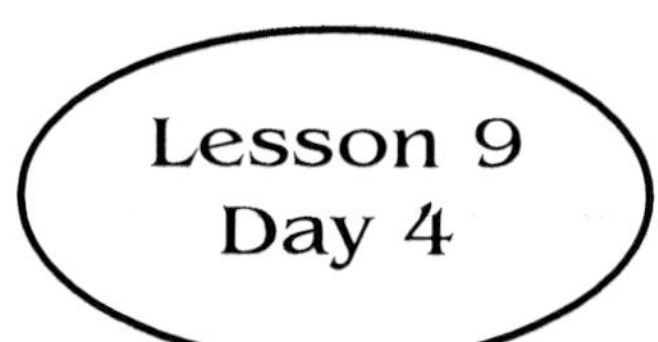

Date: _______________________

Using Adjectives

A. Look at each short sentence and picture. Cross out the **adjective** in bold and replace it with one of your own that matches the picture.

1. The **tiny** cow moos.

2. He wore a **striped** shirt.

3. We drank **sour** milk.

4. Take out the **empty** trash.

5. The **closed** book was his.

6. I used the **square** pillow.

7. I play with **round** blocks.

Date: _______________________

Using Adjectives

A. Finish the following sentences with your own **adjectives**. Use an adjective to describe the noun in bold. Make sure your **adjectives** make sense in the sentence.

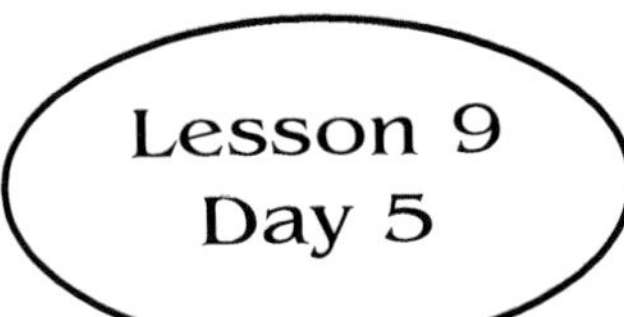

1. My sister rides a _________________________ **horse**.

2. The _________________________ **car** went by quickly.

3. The dog has a _________________________ **tail**.

4. Greg washed the _________________________ **dishes**.

5. The _________________________ **cow** grazed in the field.

6. The _________________________ **grass** looked tall.

7. The _________________________ **shirt** is ripped.

**Lesson 10
Day 1**

Using Your Senses to Describe

In the last lesson we learned how to use **adjectives** to provide the reader with more information.

I have a <u>**red**</u> blanket.

This sentence uses the adjective **red** to tell what color the blanket is. We can use **adjectives** to describe our senses (touch, sight, hearing, taste, and smell). Adjectives can tell us how a noun **feels**, **looks**, **sounds**, **tastes**, or **smells**.

On Day 1 of this lesson we will focus on **adjectives** that tell us how a noun **feels**.

I have a <u>**soft**</u> blanket.

This sentence uses the adjective **soft** to tell how the blanket feels.

The words rough, smooth, hot, cold, squishy, chewy, sticky, slimy, hard, soft, sharp, and prickly are more examples of adjectives that describe how things **feel**.

A. Finish these sentences with adjectives from the box below that describe how
the noun in bold **feels**. Use each word only once.

| prickly   hard   soft   smooth   rough   hot   sticky   scratchy |

1. The rose has _________________________ **thorns**.

2. The _________________ **stove** was dangerous.

3. The _________________ **file** is a tool.

4. The _________________ **wall** was built.

5. The flat and _________________________ **mirror** is on the desk.

6. The _________________________ **sweater** made me itch.

7. The _________________ **toy** was for the baby.

8. _________________ **syrup** is hard to clean.

Date: ______________________

Using Your
Senses to Describe

Yesterday we learned that adjectives can be used to describe things we sense. On Day 2 of this lesson we will focus on adjectives that tell how something **looks**.

The words red (all colors), round (all shapes), dark, bright, shiny, dirty, clean, high, low, large, small, nice, mean, fast, slow, and broken are examples of **adjectives** that tell how something **looks**.

A. Underline the **adjectives** in the following sentences that tell how the nouns in bold **look**.

1. The white **fence** leaned.

2. They bought a green **car**.

3. The beautiful **painting** fell.

4. Brad is a fast **runner**.

5. We sat in the bright **sun**.

6. This is a small **pencil**.

7. The large **shirt** tore.

8. The mean **dog** growled.

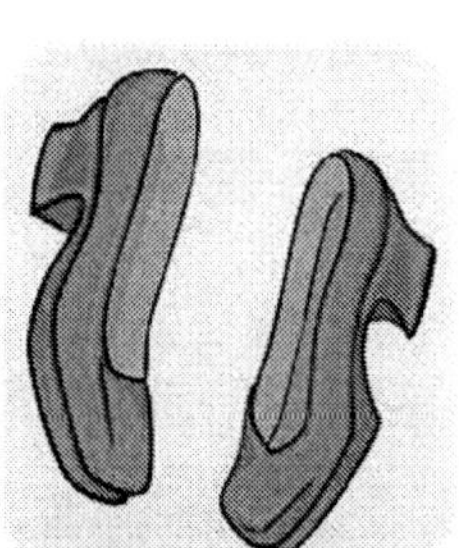

9. The red **shoes** are hers.

10. We used the shiny **forks**.

Date: ________________________

Using Your Senses to Describe

In the past couple of days we have learned that adjectives can be used to describe things we sense. So far we have covered **adjectives** that tell how something **feels** and **looks**. On Day 3 of this lesson, we will focus on adjectives that tell how something **sounds**.

The words loud, soft, squealing, squeaking, annoying, clanging, clapping, ringing, yelling, booming, crunching, crashing, ripping, and crackling are examples of **adjectives** that tell how something **sounds**.

A. Underline the **adjectives** that tell how the **noun** in bold **sounds**. Replace each of the underlined adjectives with one of your own and rewrite each sentence on the lines below.

1. We played in the crashing **waves**.

2. I heard the loud **voices**.

3. He played soft **music**.

4. Mom rang the clanging **bell**.

Date: _______________________

Using Your Senses to Describe

So far we have learned about **adjectives** that describe how things **feel**, **look**, and **sound**. Now we will focus on adjectives that tell how something **tastes**.

The words hot, cold, sour, sweet, spicy, chewy, bland, crackling, tart, crunchy, squishy, juicy, salty, disgusting, and delicious are some examples of adjectives that tell how something **tastes**.

A. Finish these sentences with adjectives from the box below that describe how the noun in bold **tastes**. Use each word only once. Remember to use capitalization when necessary.

spicy salty sour tart cold delicious sweet hot juicy crunchy

1. The _________________________ **milk** made me sick.

2. _________________________ **coffee** burns my lips.

3. The _________________________ **peas** were sweet.

4. The _________________________ **corn** was delicious.

5. The _________________________ **taco** made my tongue tingle.

6. The _________________________ **pineapple** was perfect.

7. Jim ate a _________________________ **bowl** of cereal.

8. The _________________________ **water** was refreshing.

9. The _________________________ **nuts** were her favorite.

10. He drank the _________________________ raspberry **tea**.

**Lesson 10
Day 5**

Using Your Senses to Describe

So far we have learned about **adjectives** that describe how things **feel**, **look**, **sound**, and **taste**. On Day 5 of this lesson we will focus on adjectives that tell how something **smells**.

The words smelly, sour, sweet, spicy, ripe, bitter, burning, clean, fragrant, fresh, rotten, smoky, stinky, disgusting, and delicious are some examples of adjectives that describe how something **smells**.

A. Underline the **adjectives** in the following sentences that tell how the **nouns** in bold **smell**.

1. I could smell the sweet apple **pie**.

2. I bought the delicious **pasta**.

3. The rotten **tomato** was mine.

4. Spicy **food** is my favorite.

5. Mike could smell the tart **pastry**.

6. He smelled the sour **milk**.

7. I did not eat the stinky **fish**.

8. Jeff smells his clean **shirt**.

9. He could smell the burning **logs**.

10. Dad bought fragrant **flowers**.

Using Exact Nouns

We learned in Lesson 7 that it is usually better to use a strong verb instead of a **tired** or **boring verb**. The same also applies to a noun, which of course is a **person**, **place**, or **thing**. It is better to use a more **specific noun** to name something than a **weak noun** that is more general. When we use a specific verb we call it a **strong verb**. In comparison, when we use a specific noun we call it an **exact noun**.

<u>The girl</u> gave Jim a ride.

This sentence is not very specific. It does not tell who gave Jim a ride.

<u>Shelly</u> gave Jim a ride.

This sentence is much more exact because it provides the reader with a clearer image of who actually gave Jim a ride.

A. Read each group of words and underline the **exact nouns** for each word in bold.

1. **seat -** couch, recliner, pants, chair

2. **music -** jazz, telephone, classical, country

3. **container -** pan, glass, blanket, can

4. **food -** cheese, book, bread, pencil

5. **tool -** wrench, screwdriver, shoe, box

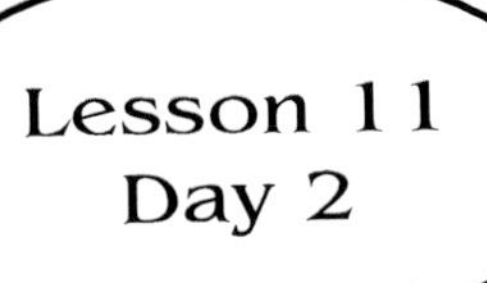

**Lesson 11
Day 2**

Using Exact Nouns

A. Read each pair of sentences. Write an **X** next to the sentence in each pair that has an **exact noun**.

1. a. ____ Keri watched the show.

   b. ____ The girl watched the show.

2. a. ____ The tool broke.

   b. ____ The hammer broke.

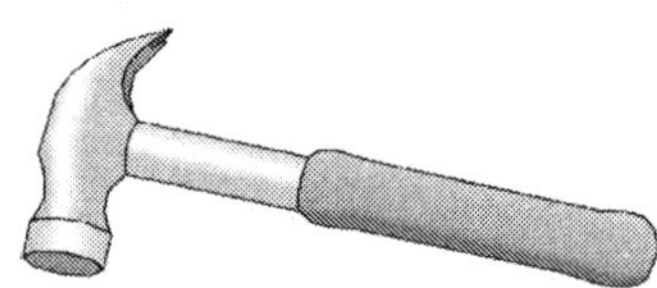

3. a. ____ The song was good.

   b. ____ The ballad was good.

4. a. ____ The alligator bit me!

   b. ____ The animal bit me!

5. a. ____ The seat was warm.

   b. ____ The couch was warm.

6. a. ____ The spotlight made it easier to read.

   b. ____ The light made it easier to read.

7. a. ____ The boy tried to help me.

   b. ____ George tried to help me.

8. a. ____ The fly kept buzzing.

   b. ____ The insect kept buzzing.

9. a. ____ The woman swam in the pool.

   b. ____ Sandra swam in the pool.

10. a. ____ Captain Smith helped me cross the road.

   b. ____ The policeman helped me cross the road.

Using Exact Nouns

A. Read each pair of sentences below. The first sentence in each pair contains a **weak noun** that you will underline. Complete the second sentence of each pair by inserting an **exact noun** from the box below to replace the weak noun in the first sentence.

top	bear	Gail	chair	folder
pitcher	soup	house	corn	band

1. a. The animal crept into our yard.

    b. The _________________ crept into our yard.

2. a. We hold school in the building.

    b. We hold school in the _________________.

3. a. The seat was comfortable.

    b. The _________________ was comfortable.

4. a. The toy spun.

    b. The _________________ spun.

5. a. The food was hot and tasty.

   b. The _________________________ was hot and tasty.

6. a. The girl was ready for school.

   b. _________________________ was ready for school.

7. The plant was harvested.

   The _________________________ was harvested.

8. The case held the papers.

   The _________________________ held the papers.

9. The group was loud!

   The _________________________ was loud!

10. The container held iced tea.

   The _________________________ held iced tea.

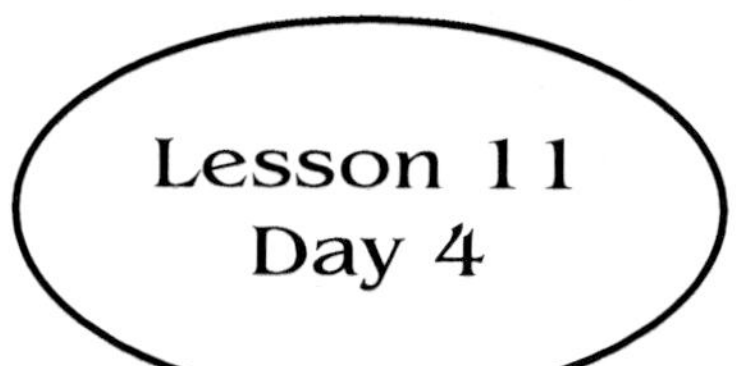

Date: ______________________

Using Exact Nouns

A. Read the sentences below and insert an **exact noun** from the box below. Use each word only once. Remember to use correct capitalization when necessary.

novel	pie
rose	pool
oatmeal	dentist
peanuts	Alice
unicycle	beach

1. The _________________________ grew until it blossomed.

2. Did _________________ eat the last doughnut?

3. The _________________ fixed my tooth.

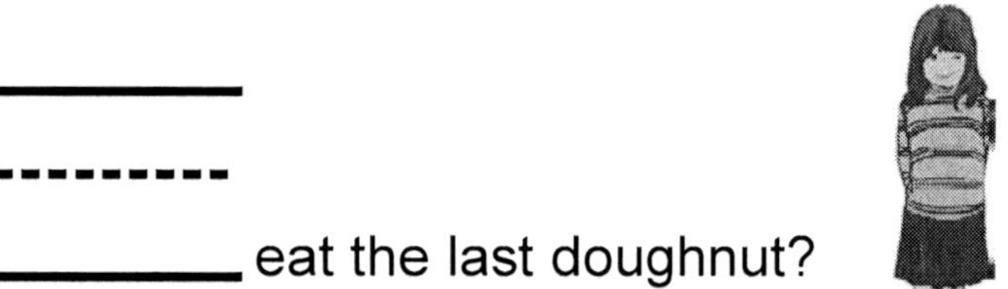

4. The _________________ about the South was interesting.

5. A _________________________ was prepared by the chef.

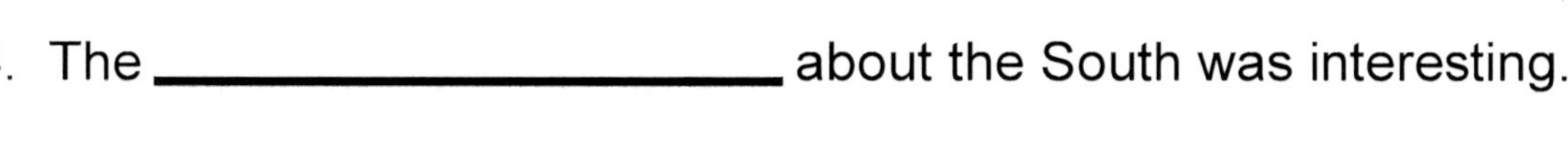

6. We played on the _________________________ all day.

7. _________________________ is good for breakfast.

8. The _________________________ was a fun place to swim.

9. The salty _________________________ were her favorite.

10. The _________________________ was very hard to ride.

Using Exact Nouns

A. Read the following sentences. Five **weak nouns** have been underlined.
Write each **weak noun** on the lines below and then write an **exact noun** next
to it that could take its place in the sentence. Use your own exact nouns.

I play <u>sports</u> with the <u>boy</u> and the <u>girl</u>. I try to hit the <u>object</u> with a bat. We eat <u>food</u> when we are finished.

Weak Nouns	Exact Nouns
1. a. _______________	1. b. _______________
2. a. _______________	2. b. _______________
3. a. _______________	3. b. _______________
4. a. _______________	4. b. _______________
5. a. _______________	5. b. _______________

Review of Using Strong Verbs

A. Finish these sentences with a **strong verb** from the box below. Use each verb only once.

fluttered	shook	dashed	tossed	cooked
flooded	steamed	strolled	pounced	rolled

1. The lamp _____________ the stage with light.

2. Mom ___________ the vegetables.

3. Mike ___________ across the street.

4. The boy ___________ across the finish line.

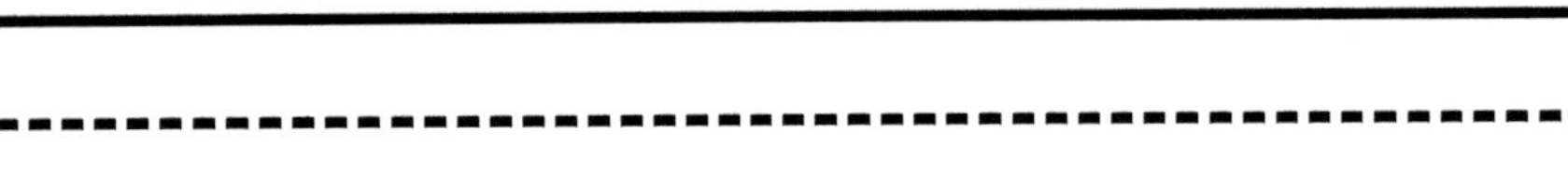

5. Joshua ___________ the ball.

6. The bird ____________.

7. The cat ____________.

8. The thunder ____________ the house.

9. The car ____________ through the stoplight.

10. The pot of soup ____________ on the stove.

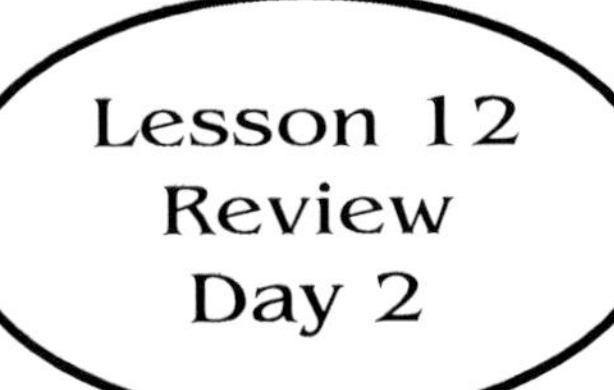

Review of Describing the Action

A. Write the **adverb** that sounds better in each sentence.

1. **today**, **always**

   ____

   -

   We ________________________ eat healthy foods.

2. **sadly**, **slowly**

   ____

   -

   The horse ________________________ galloped.

3. **carefully**, **yesterday**

   ____

   -

   He ________________________ ate all of his lunch.

4. **heavily**, **loudly**

   ____

   -

   It snowed ________________________ .

5. **always**, **outside**

   ____

   -

   We played ________________________ for a while.

6. **never**, **neatly**

____

- -

We _______________________ jump off a ladder.

7. **lightly**, **bravely**

____

- -

Nellie _______________________ skipped the jump rope.

8. **angrily**, **quietly**

____

- -

Dan _______________________ read the story.

Review of Using Adjectives

A. Look at the pictures below. Write an **adjective**(descriptive word) and a **noun** (naming word) for each picture. Use the words in the boxes below.

<u>Adjectives</u>

swift	mad	spinning
hot	tall	hissing

<u>Nouns</u>

building	snake	hornet
top	fire	river

1.

2.

3.

4.

5.

6.

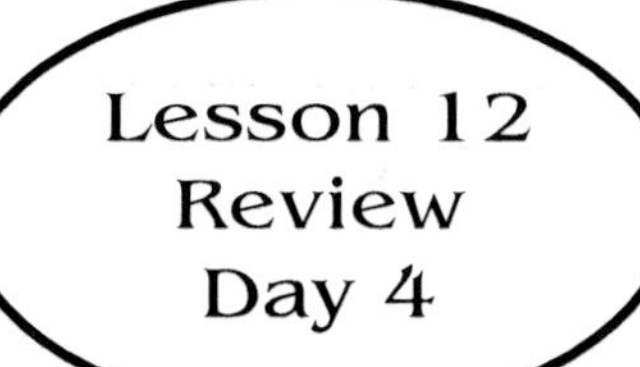

Review of Using Your Senses to Describe

A. Finish the following sentences with **adjectives** that describe how things **sound**, **taste**, **feel**, **look**, or **smell**. Choose your own adjectives to finish each sentence. Make sure your adjectives make sense.

1. We could smell the _________________________ cheese.

2. The _________________ music hurt my ears.

3. The _________________ sandpaper scraped off the old paint.

4. I ate the _________________ tomato.

5. We could barely hear the_________________________ whispers.

6. The _________________________ shirt felt good on my skin.

7. I ate the _________________________ pastry.

8. The _________________________ perfume was nice.

9. The _________________________ nuts were her favorite.

10. The _________________________ day was good for sailing.

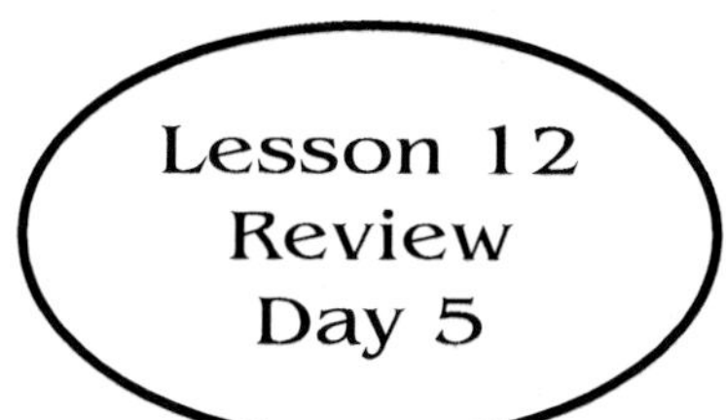

Date: ___________________________

Review of Using Exact Nouns

A. Read each pair of sentences below. The first sentence in each pair contains a **weak noun** that is underlined. Complete the second sentence of the pair by inserting an **exact noun** to replace the weak noun in the first sentence.

1. The <u>box</u> held the documents.

   ____

   -

   The ________________________________ held the documents.

2. The <u>vessel</u> held the water.

   ____

   -

   The ________________________________ held the water.

3. The <u>plants</u> were pretty.

   ____

   -

   The ________________________________ were pretty.

4. Henry plays <u>sports</u>.

   ____

   -

   Henry plays ________________________________.

5. Jessie wanted some <u>food</u>.

   ____

   -

   Jessie wanted some ________________________________.

6. The <u>animal</u> was barking.

____

- -

The_______________________________ was barking.

7. The <u>fruit</u> was sweet and delicious.

____

- -

The _______________________________ was sweet and delicious.

8. The <u>creature</u> played in the tree.

____

- -

The _______________________________ played in the tree.

9. The <u>people</u> raced.

____

- -

The _______________________________ raced.

10. His <u>clothes</u> were a bit loose.

____

- -

His _______________________________ were a bit loose.

Date: _______________________

Introduction to Topics

All stories start with the writer choosing a **topic**. A **topic** is very similar to the title of a book because it tells the reader what the story is about. Let's assume we want to write a story about **animals**. We would first choose a topic about the type of animal we want in our story. Then, we would write sentences for our story that talk about that type of animal.

It is very useful to have a topic before we start writing. Having a topic keeps the writer focused on the story. If you have selected the topic of **alligators**, then your story should not include sentences that talk about other types of animals unless the other animals are somehow related to the story. For example, you might want to write about the types of food alligators eat.

A. Underline the most appropriate topic for each type of story below.

1. a story about penguins and their babies

    - arctic birds
    - penguins
    - penguins and their young
    - animals in the cold

2. a story about toys in your room

    - furniture in my house
    - my room of toys
    - things under my bed
    - games I like to play

Date: ________________________

Introduction to Topics

A. Look at each picture below. Underline the topic under each picture that best describes the picture.

1.   sports
playing basketball
great athletes

3.   fun hobbies
things to make
making pottery

2.   big cats
animals in Africa
lions

4. my favorite planet
Saturn is interesting
planets far away

Introduction to Topics

Read the following four sentences.

Puppies like to run and play.

Puppies are fun to have.

My puppy loves treats.

Puppies need to be potty trained.

To determine if there is a common **topic** among these four sentences, go back and read each sentence again. Is there anything that all of the sentences have in common? The first sentence talks about how puppies like to run and play. The second sentence mentions that puppies are fun to have. The third sentence tells that the puppy loves treats. Finally, the fourth sentence discusses how puppies need to be potty trained. Each of the four sentences is related to puppies. Therefore, we can determine that **puppies** could be the topic of these four sentences.

A. Read the four sentences below. Do they have a common topic?

I like riding horses.

Horses are often friendly.

You should use a saddle when you ride a horse.

Horses are the most fun when they run.

Write the topic on the line.

1. _______________________

Date: _______________________

Introduction to Topics

A. Do the following pictures match the **topics** written next to them? Write **yes** or **no** on each line.

1.  = dancing together

2.  = car racing

3.  = walking

4.  = sleeping

5.  = men singing

6.  = dog walking

Lesson 13
Day 5

Introduction to Topics

A. Look at these pictures. Write a short **topic** for each picture below.

1.______________________________

4.______________________________

2.______________________________

5.______________________________

3.______________________________

6.______________________________

Date:_______________________

Thinking of Ideas for a Story

Now that you know how to select a topic for a story, you will see how easy it is to come up with ideas for your story.

Let's assume we have selected for our story the topic of **how to pick an apple from a tree**. Now that we have a topic, we need to think of some ideas to put in our story.

Let's start by thinking of steps necessary **to pick an apple from a tree**.

- find an apple tree
- get a ladder
- climb the tree
- find a apple that is ripe
- pick the apple from the branch

Are these good ideas for a story about picking an apple from a tree? Yes, because they all tell about steps necessary to pick an apple.

A. Assume that we have a topic of **how to build a dog house**. Write an **X** next to the ideas that could fit in this story.

1. _____ buy the correct amount of wood and nails

2. _____ design the doghouse on paper

3. _____ buy a dog

4. _____ correctly saw the wood into pieces

5. _____ build the doghouse

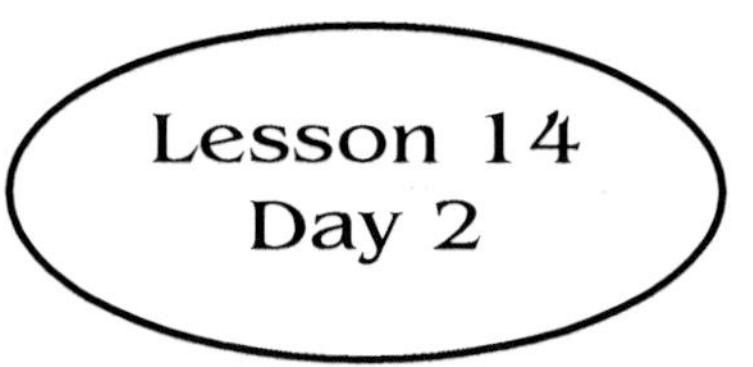

Date:________________________

Thinking of Ideas
for a Story

A. Look at the pictures below. Underline the ideas that could go into a story about each picture.

1. It is Adam's birthday.
It is getting dark.
He loves birthday cake.
I had peas for lunch.

3. Skating is fun.
I wear a helmet.
I get a drink of water.
I try not to fall.

2. I like to row the boat.
Rowing is hard work.
I like to climb trees.
I race other boaters.

4. Painting is relaxing.
I spilled paint.
I use pretty colors.
I paint often.

**Lesson 14
Day 3**

Thinking of Ideas for a Story

A. A boy named **Tommy** is writing a story about **his dog named Millie**. He has listed five ideas below that he thinks would be good for his story. There is one idea that really does not belong in his story. Cross out the idea that really does not belong.

Topic: **I like my dog**

1. I like Millie because she is large.

2. I like Millie because she likes to cuddle and lick my face.

3. Once I also had a hamster.

4. Millie likes to play fetch.

5. I also like the color of Millie's fur.

B. Can you think of another reason Tommy might like Millie? Write it on the lines below.

1.

Date:________________

Thinking of Ideas
for a Story

A. Mary is writing a story about **places where I would like to travel**. She has already thought of four ideas, but she needs your help. Write two more ideas for her.

- I would like to travel to Hawaii.
- I have always wanted to go to Ireland.
- I would like to see the Grand Canyon.
- I would like to play on a beach someday.

1.

2.

Date:_______________________

Thinking of Ideas for a Story

A. Below is a story about **making a glass of water to drink**. There are several steps or ideas in this story. Write two of the steps on the lines below.

When I get thirsty

When I get thirsty I want a nice cool glass of water to drink. First, I get a clean glass from the cupboard and place it under the faucet. Next, I turn the faucet on and fill the glass half full. Then, I put ice cubes in the glass. Finally, I take the glass to the kitchen table and drink it.

1.

2.

**Lesson 15
Day 1**

Putting It in Order

In the last lesson we learned how to think of ideas for a story by focusing on a **topic**. In this lesson we will learn that not only do we need to think of ideas for a story, but also we often need to organize those ideas in a certain order.

For example, suppose we want to write a story about **how to draw a picture**. In order to get started we have written five ideas for our story below.

-Color the picture.

-Place a piece of paper on the table.

-Decide what to draw.

-Draw the picture.

-Place markers on the table.

If you look closely you will see that these ideas are steps for drawing a picture. Are they in the correct order? No, they are not. A logical organization of the steps might look like the following:

1. Decide what to draw.
2. Place a piece of paper on the table.
3. Place markers on the table.
4. Draw the picture.
5. Color the picture.

You could add more detail to this list, but this example shows you that there is often an order that must be followed when telling a story.

A. Below are four steps showing **how to pick an apple from a tree**, but they
are not in the correct order. Place the numbers **1** through **4** next to the steps
below to place them in the correct order.

1.______ Pick the apple from the branch.

2.______ Find an apple tree.

3.______ Climb the tree.

4.______ When you find a tree, find a apple that is ripe.

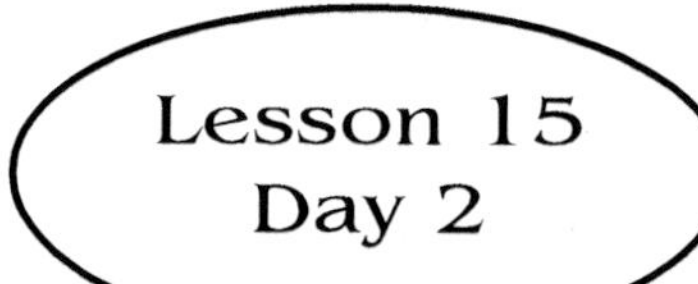

Date:_______________

Putting It in Order

A. The sentences below represent the ideas or steps for **making a glass of ice water**. Put them in the correct order by placing the numbers **1** through **4** on the lines.

1.______ Put ice cubes into the glass of water.

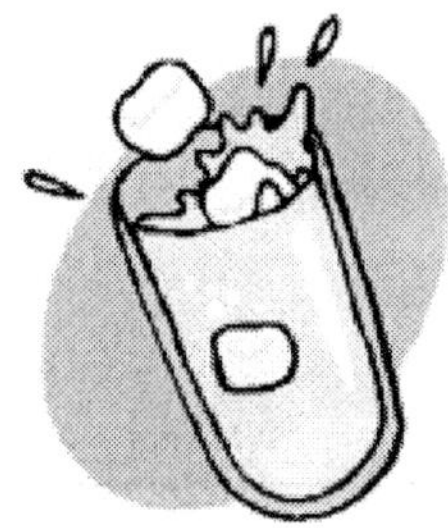

2.______ Remove a clean glass from the cupboard.

3.______ Turn the faucet on and fill the glass half full.

4.______ Place the empty glass under the faucet.

B. The sentences below represent the steps for **making a paper airplane**. Put them in the correct order by placing the numbers **1** through **4** on the lines.

1.______ Fly the airplane.

2.______ Get a piece of paper.

3.______ Place a paper clip on the folded airplane for balance.

4.______ Fold the paper into the shape of the desired airplane.

Date:_______________

Putting It in Order

When we write short stories we usually begin the sentences of the story with introductory words like **first**, **next**, **then**, and **finally**.

Here is a short sample story about a girl getting ready to ride her bike.

First, I put on my elbow and knee pads. **Next**, I put my helmet on my head. **Then**, I get my bike out of the garage. **Finally**, I get on my bike and ride.

A. Below are the four ideas you arranged on Day 2 showing **how to make a paper airplane**. They should be in this order:

- Get a piece of paper.
- Fold the paper into the shape of the desired airplane.
- Place a paper clip on the folded airplane for balance.
- Fly the airplane.

We are going to write a story with these four ideas. Place the introductory words **first**, **next**, **then**, and **finally** in the blanks.

1.___________________________, get a piece of paper.

2.___________________________, fold the paper into the shape of an airplane.

3.___________________________, put a paper clip on the folded airplane for balance.

4.___________________________, fly the airplane.

Putting It in Order

A. Let's write another story. Linda would like to write a story about **riding her horse**. She has thought of the four ideas below for her story.

- Get on the horse.
- Put the saddle and bridle on the horse.
- Ride the horse.
- Get the horse out of the barn by using the bridle.

Put the below ideas in the correct order by placing the numbers **1** through **4** on the lines.

1._____ Get on the horse.

2._____ Put the saddle and bridle on the horse.

3._____ Ride the horse.

4._____ Get the horse out of the barn by using the bridle.

B. We have taken the ideas from the last page and arranged them into a story.
Place the introductory words **first**, **next**, **then**, and **finally** on the lines.
Remember to use correct capitalization.

1.__________________________, put the saddle and bridle on the horse.

2.__________________________, get the horse out of the barn by using the

bridle.

3.__________________________, get on the horse.

4.__________________________, ride the horse.

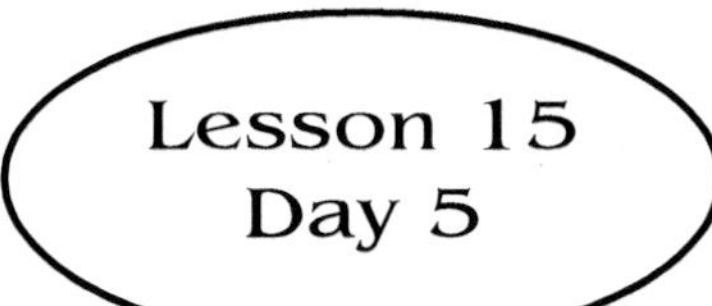

Date:_______________________

Putting It in Order

A. Dad would like to write a story about **going for a ride in the car**. So far he has thought of the three ideas below for his story. Can you think of a fourth idea that would be the last part of his story? Write it on the line below.

- I start the car.

- I grab my car keys.

- I walk out of the house.

B. Put the above ideas in the correct order by placing the correct number on each line (steps 1-3) below. Also, add your idea below. It will be what happens last in the story.

1. _____ I start the car.

2. _____ I grab my car keys.

3. _____ I walk out of the house.

4. 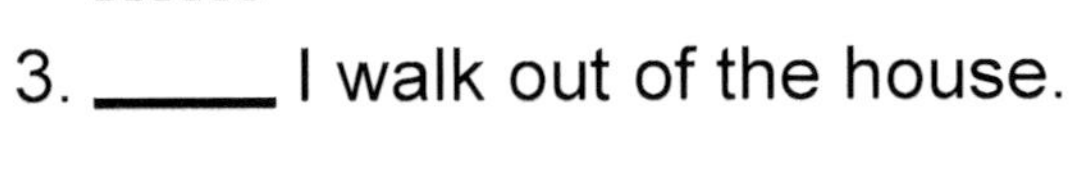

C. We have taken the ideas from the last page and arranged them into a story. Place the introductory words **first**, **next**, **then**, and **finally** on the lines. Don't forget to add your idea below. Remember to use correct capitalization.

____

1.________________________, I grab my car keys.

2.________________________, I walk out of the house.

3.________________________, I start the car.

4.________________________,

Lesson 16
Day 1

Beginning, Middle, and Ending

So far we have learned how to make interesting sentences and how to connect them together to tell a short story. In this lesson we will learn that when we write a story it must have a **beginning**, **middle**, and an **ending**.

The beginning sentence of a story is called an **introductory sentence** and its purpose is to tell what the story is about. Another purpose of the introductory sentence is to gain the interest of the reader. With this in mind, we must make the introductory sentence as exciting as possible.

For example, in which story would you have more interest?

Doug went to the store.

-or-

Doug jumped into his rocket ship and blasted off to the store.

The second sentence is much more interesting since it provides much more detail to the story.

A. Read each pair of **introductory sentences** below. Write an **X** on the line next to the most interesting sentence of each pair.

1. a. ____ We baked a cake.

   b. ____ Mom and I baked a two level birthday cake for Sammy.

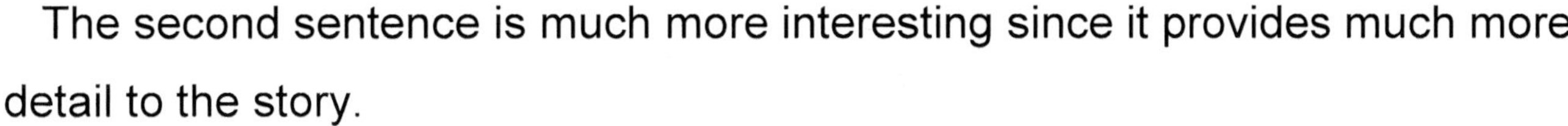

2. a. ____ We drove to the beach.

   b. ____ We drove the convertible to the beach while our favorite music played.

3. a.____ The cat was angry.

   b. ____ The tiger was angry and ready to attack!

4. a.____ The frigid water was so deep we could not see the bottom.

   b. ____ The water was deep.

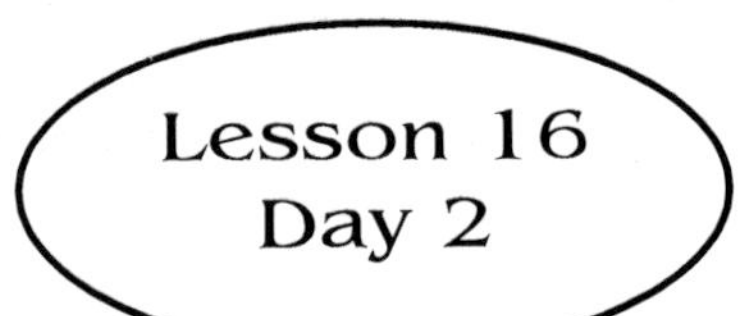

Beginning, Middle, and Ending

Now that we know how to start a story with an interesting introductory sentence, we also need to learn how to write a good story (the **middle**).

We learned back in Lesson 15 to use words like **first**, **next**, **then**, and **last** to describe the order of details as they appear in a story. **However, if there is no particular order required to tell the story, these introductory words are not needed**.

As you've probably figured out by now, the middle portion of the story is based on the **ideas** (Lesson 14) you listed after focusing on your **topic**. Of course this means that the middle portion of your story has to be related to what was discussed in the introductory sentence.

A. Read the sentences below. Write an **X** next to each sentence that belongs in a story about **sharks**.

1. ____ They constantly swim and hunt.

2. ____ They live on land.

3. ____ They have very sharp teeth.

4. ____ These animals do not eat meat.

5. ____ They are just as comfortable on land as they are in the water.

6. ____ They have fins and a tail.

Date:_______________

Beginning, Middle, and Ending

So far in this lesson we have learned to start the **beginning** of a story with an exciting introductory sentence. We also learned to write an interesting **middle** portion of the story that is related to the introductory sentence. Now all we need to learn is how to write a good **ending sentence** to the story.

A good ending sentence is one that summarizes what happened in the story. An ending sentence can also be one that concludes or ties together what happened throughout the story. A good ending sentence can also answer one or more questions that were raised during the story.

A. Read the following story that does **not** have an ending sentence. Write an **X** next to the **ending** that is the best for this story.

Title: **The Missing Shoes**

One morning my favorite pair of shoes was missing. I could not find my shoes anywhere. I was so upset. I looked in the closet, and I looked in the hall. I even looked in my room. I was shocked that my shoes had disappeared. I gave up after looking for fifteen minutes. I finally figured out that...

1.____ Mom had made cookies for us.

2.____ we were all confused by the missing shoes.

3.____ my dog Charlie took my shoes to chew on them.

4.____ I could have looked many other places but didn't.

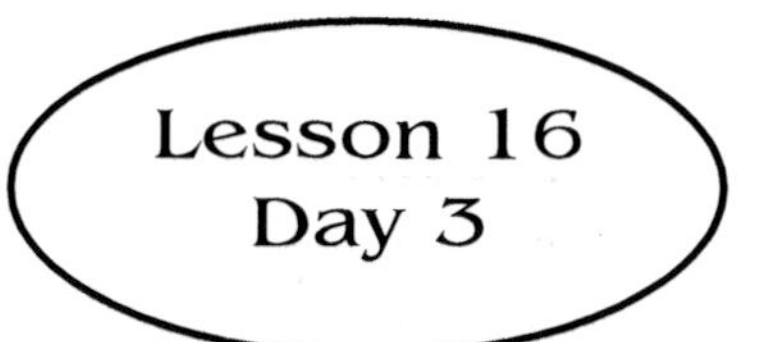

Date:_______________

Beginning, Middle, and Ending

A. A title to a story has been provided below. The middle portion of the story has also been provided. You need to write a good **introductory sentence** and a good **ending sentence** to the story on the lines below.

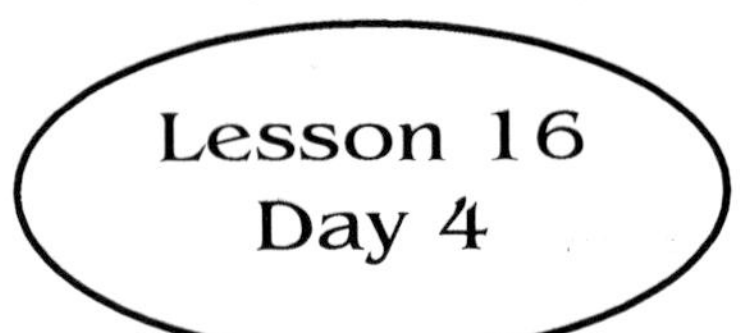

Title: My Favorite Book

1. Introductory sentence: ________________________

The book about the astronaut makes me wish I were in outer space. I imagine wearing a spacesuit and walking in space. This book makes me want to walk on the moon someday.

2. Ending sentence: ________________________

**Lesson 16
Day 5**

Beginning, Middle, and Ending

A. A title to a story has been provided below. The middle portion of the story has also been provided. You need to write a good **introductory sentence** and a good **ending sentence** to the story on the lines below. The **introductory sentence** has been started for you.

Title: My Favorite Sport

____

1. My favorite sport to play is_______________________________

____

____

I enjoy playing this sport because it is fun. It gives me a lot of exercise. I also enjoy playing it with my friends.

____

2. Ending sentence: _______________________________

____

____

____

____

____

Grouping Ideas and Details

In previous lessons we learned that a good **story** has to have an **interesting beginning**, **middle**, and **ending**.

Since the middle portion of the story is the largest of the three parts, it is very important that this section includes interesting sentences (with a lot of detail). It is equally important that the middle portion of the story be well organized by grouping together common ideas and details. If you fail to do this, your story will likely be very confusing to the reader.

A. Read the following story. The details in the middle portion of the story are not well organized. Cross out the sentence that does not belong in this group of ideas and details.

Title: Breakfast

I always eat breakfast because it is the most important meal of the day for me. Eating a good breakfast gives me energy and gets me going in the morning. Sometimes the telephone rings at night during dinner. I usually eat pancakes or waffles for breakfast. If I am in a hurry, then I eat toast. Breakfast makes me feel good and helps me start the day.

Can you see how this story is a little confusing to the reader since it has a sentence that is not really related to the other sentences in the story?

Date:_______________________

Grouping Ideas and Details

When we write a story it makes sense to keep ideas together that are related.

A. Read the sentences below. Write an **X** next to each sentence that belongs in the group. Can you tell what the story is about?

1. ____ I heated the oven to 375 degrees.

2. ____ I let the dog outside.

3. ____ I mixed the flour, sugar, and yeast together.

4. ____ I made myself a glass of lemonade.

5. ____ I poured the batter into a pan.

6. ____ I placed the batter-filled pan in the oven.

7. ____ I used a knife to spread frosting on the baked good.

B. What would be a good **title** for this story? Write it below. Remember to use correct capitalization.

1. ________________________________

**Lesson 17
Day 3**

Grouping Ideas
and Details

A. Read the sentences below. Write an **X** next to each sentence that belongs in the group. Can you tell what the story is about?

1. ____ I sharpen the blade.

2. ____ I pull the mower out of the garage.

3. ____ I talk to my neighbor.

4. ____ I fill the mower with gas.

5. ____ I waxed my car.

6. ____ I start the mower.

7. ____ I mow in circles around the lawn.

B. What would be a good **title** for this story? Write it below.

1. ________________________________

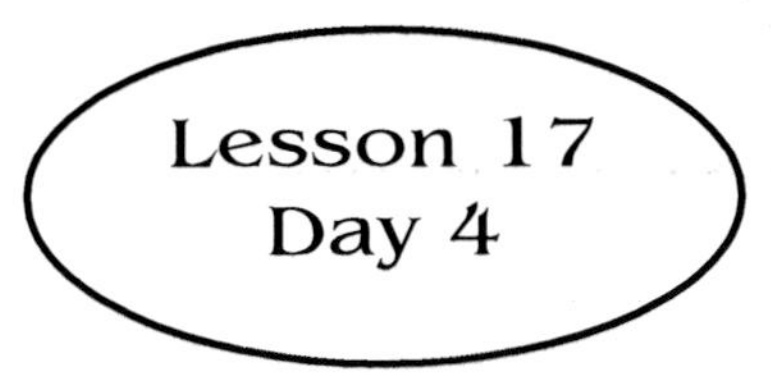

Grouping Ideas and Details

A. Read the sentences in the boxes below. Cross out the ideas that do not belong in a group that matches each picture.

1.

The hockey puck is hard.	A hockey stick is needed.
I wear a helmet.	I scored two goals.
Ice skate blades are sharp.	I do not like baseball.
I get hungry after I play football.	I need to do my homework.

2.

I grow carrots in my garden	I harvest the carrots that are ready.
Rabbits eat my carrots.	It is cold outside.
I bought a skateboard last year.	I get dirty in the garden.
My family eats the garden food.	I also grow lettuce.

Date:________________

Grouping Ideas and Details

A. Below is a group of ideas that are related to **cooking and eating spaghetti**. Can you think of two more ideas that would also fit into this group?

- I make a sauce with tomatoes.
- I boil some noodles.
- I make meatballs.
- I set the table.
- I get everyone a napkin and fork.

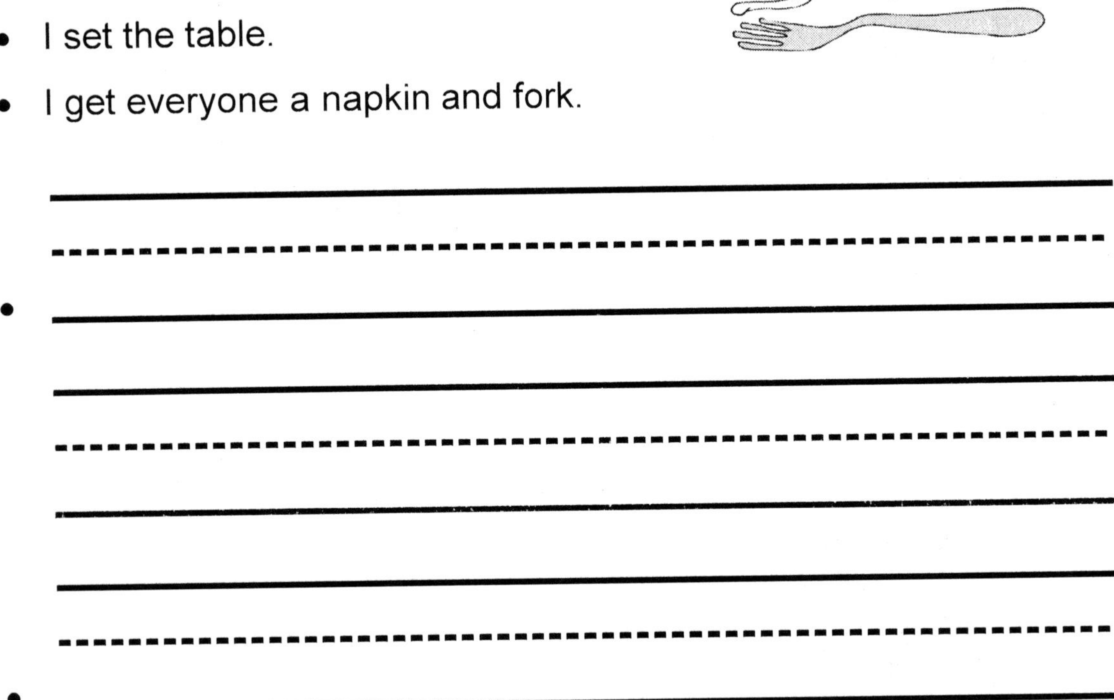

Date:_______________

Review of Introduction to Topics

A. Underline the most appropriate topic for each type of story below.

1. a story about lions and their babies
   - big cats of Africa
   - candy stores in Africa
   - hotels in Africa
   - sleeping habits of bats

2. types of furniture
   - a pair of shoes
   - a book
   - a couch
   - a cat

3. types of television shows
   - comedy
   - pickles
   - pictures
   - cold

4. types of clothing
   - chair
   - pants
   - cup
   - swing

Date:_______________

Review of Thinking of Ideas for a Story

A. Look at these pictures. Write a short **topic** for each picture below.

1.______________________

2.______________________

3.______________________

4.______________________

5.______________________

6.______________________

Date:______________________

Review of Putting It in Order

A. Bill would like to write a **story**. He has thought of the four ideas below for his story.

- I spread sauce on the crust.
- I spread cheese on the crust and sauce.
- I spread the dough on the pizza pan to make a crust.
- I place the meat toppings on the cheese.

Put the ideas above in the correct **order** by placing the numbers **1** through **4** on the lines below.

1._____ I spread sauce on the crust.

2._____ I spread cheese on the crust and sauce.

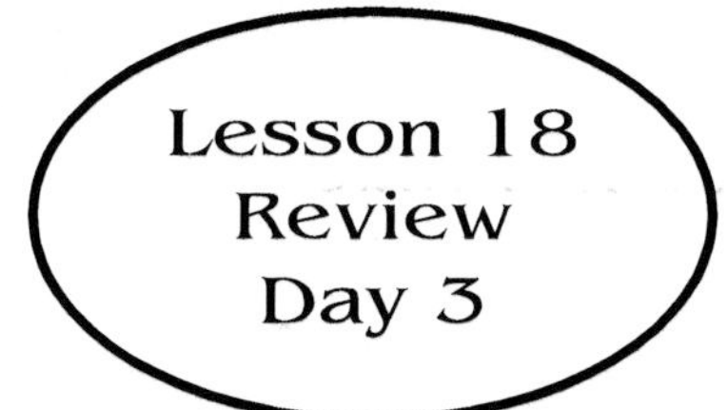

3._____ I spread the dough on the pizza pan to make a crust.

4._____ I place the meat toppings on the cheese.

B. Write a good **topic** for the above story.

1.____

Date:________________

Review of Beginning, Middle, and Ending

A. Read the sentences below. Write an **X** next to each sentence that belongs in a story about **giraffes**.

1. ___ Giraffes are tall.

2. ___ Giraffes do not eat meat.

3. ___ Giraffes have a spotted coat.

4. ___ Giraffes have short necks.

5. ___ Giraffes have long legs.

6. ___ Giraffes live mainly in Canada.

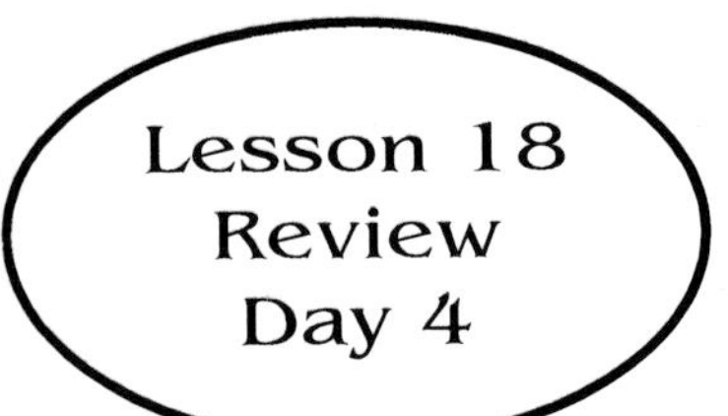

B. Read the sentences below. Write an **X** next to each sentence that belongs in a story about the **weather**.

1. ___ Sometimes in rains in the spring.

2. ___ It gets very hot in the summer.

3. ___ It could snow if it is hot outside.

4. ___ Thunder can be very loud.

5. ___ Snow is hot.

6. ___ We can wear shorts when it snows.

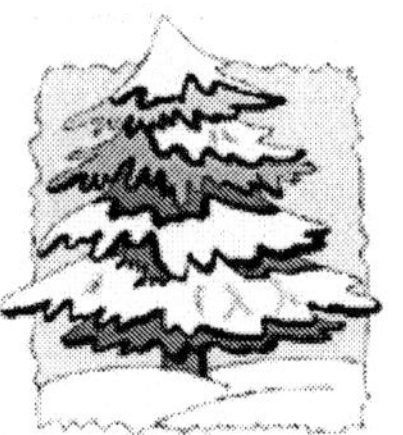

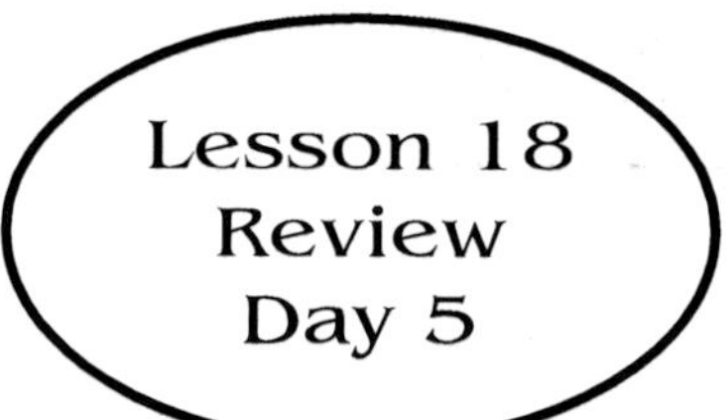

Date:_______________

Review of Grouping Ideas and Details

A. Below is a group of ideas that are related to **going to the beach**. Can you think of two more ideas that would also fit into this group?

- I take a towel.
- I put on sun block.
- I take a picnic lunch.
- I wear swimming trunks.
- I bring an umbrella to block the sun.

Date:_______________________

Grouping Same and Different

In Lesson 17 we learned about grouping **common** ideas and details together within a story. Sometimes it is good to include details in your stories that are similar, sometimes it is not. It really depends on the type of story you are writing.

When is something **different** when compared to something else? It depends on the question asked, doesn't it?

For example, let's pretend that we have a group of people standing in front of us who are basketball players. Are they different?

It depends. Are they different heights? Are they on different teams? Are some male and some female? Do they have different color hair?

You can see that depending on the question asked, the answer may be different. With this in mind, look at the two pictures below. Are they the same or different?

It depends. If the question is whether or not they are both athletes, then the answer is that they are the **same** because they are both athletes. If the question is whether or not they play the same sport, then the answer is that they are **different** because one plays football and one plays baseball.

A. Look at the pictures below. On the lines, write two ways that these two people are the same and two ways that they are different.

1. **Same**

a. ____

b. ____

2. **Different**

a. ____

b. ____

Date:_______________________

Grouping Same and Different

A. Assume we are writing a general story about **athletes**. From the list below, write an **X** on the line next to the details that would be appropriate to include in this story.

1. ____ people who do not like sports

2. ____ babies

3. ____ baseball players

4. ____ hockey players

5. ____ runners

6. ____ football players

7. ____ soccer players

B. Assume we are writing a story that includes **athletes** who play a sport that uses a **ball**. Using the same list from above, write an **X** on the line next to the details that would be appropriate to include in this story.

1. ____ people who do not like sports

2. ____ babies

3. ____ baseball players

4. ____ hockey players

5. ____ runners

6. ____ football players

7. ____ soccer players

Grouping Same and Different

A. Assume we are writing a story about how **basketball players** are **different** from **football players**. Using the list below, write an **X** on the line next to the details that would be appropriate to include in this story.

1. ____ basketball players do not wear a helmet, but football players do

2. ____ football players use a ball that has pointy ends and basketball players use a ball that is round

3. ____ football players tackle their opponents but basketball players do not

4. ____ both are athletes

5. ____ both wear uniforms

6. ____ football players wear shoulder pads, but basketball players do not

7. ____ playing both requires each team member to run

B. Assume we are writing a story about how **cats** are **different** from **dogs**. Using the list below, write an **X** on the line next to the details that would be appropriate to include in this story.

1. ____ both have four legs

2. ____ dogs bark, but cats purr

3. ____ cats can climb trees, but dogs cannot

4. ____ both have sharp teeth

5. ____ cats use a litter box, but dogs do not

6. ____ cats are related to tigers, but dogs are not

7. ____ both have claws

Date:________________

Grouping Same and Different

A. A **title** to a story has been provided below. The **introductory** and **ending** sentences of the story have also been provided. Write three sentences that give more information on this topic. Make sure your sentences are well organized and match the **title** of the story.

Title: How all Trees are the Same

All trees are plants and have many similar features.

For the reasons stated above, all trees share many features and therefore are the same in many ways.

**Lesson 19
Day 5**

Date:___________________

Grouping Same and Different

A. A **title** to a story has been provided below. Write an **introductory** sentence, a **three sentence** middle portion that tells more about the topic, and an **ending** sentence.

Title: How Summer is Different from Winter

Describing Things

Date:______________________

In Lesson 9 we learned how **adjectives** describe **nouns** and make sentences more interesting to read. In this lesson we will concentrate on describing people, places, and things in greater detail.

This is a picture of girl eating ice cream, but are there any other words we could use to describe her or what she is doing?

We could list the following details:

-She has a balloon in her hand.

-She is wearing a pointy hat.

-She is licking an ice cream cone.

-She has dark hair.

As you will see, being able to describe things in greater detail will help you write more interesting sentences.

A. Look at this picture. From the list below, write an <u>X</u> on the line next to each
   detail that could be used to describe what you see in the picture.

1. ____   There is a storm cloud in the sky.

2. ____   Her puppy likes to watch.

3. ____   The girl is wearing short pants.

4. ____   The girl has her hair in a pony tail.

5. ____   She is riding on a lawnmower.

6. ____   It is snowing.

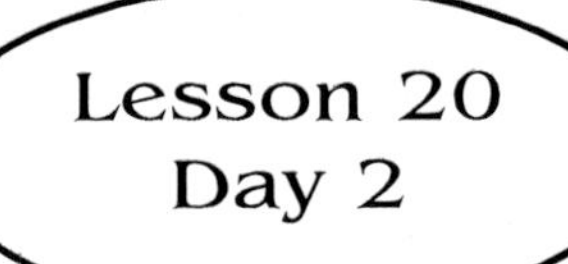

Describing Things

A. Look at the pictures below. From the list below, write an **X** on the line next to each detail that could be used to describe what you see in each picture.

1. a. ____ This man is mad.

   b. ____ His computer monitor is broken.

   c. ____ He is wearing a hat.

   d. ____ The computer screen is smoking.

   e. ____ The man is sitting in a chair.

   f. ____ He is wearing a tie.

2. a. ____ This boy is hungry.

   b. ____ His burger is dripping.

   c. ____ He is sleeping.

   d. ____ The boy is using both hands to eat.

   e. ____ The boy is laughing.

   f. ____ The boy is licking his lips.

Describing Things

Date:____________________

Look at this picture.

Here are some sentences that describe what is happening in the picture.

- The clown has a pointy hat on his nose.
- The clown has big shoes.
- The clown has a fake nose on his head.
- The clown has many colorful shapes on his coat.

Below is a sentence that describes the clown.

The clown wore a silly hat and a fake nose.

Compare the above sentence to the sentence below.

The clown with the colorful coat and big shoes wore a

fake nose on his head and a pointy hat on his nose.

Can you see how much more interesting the second sentence is compared to the first? If someone were describing the clown to you (without showing you the picture), think of how much more you would learn about the clown from the second sentence.

A. Look at this picture. You will find three details below that describe the picture.
Write a sentence using all or parts of the three details to describe the picture.

- The flowers are on a table.
- The flowers are colorful.
- The flowers are in a vase.

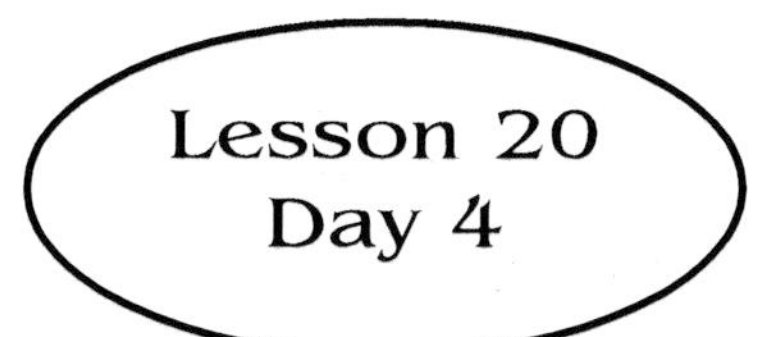

Describing Things

A. Look at the picture below. First, add another **descriptive** detail to describe the picture on the first line below. (Hint: What is he wearing on his head?) Next, use at least two of the three details, including the one you added, to write a sentence to describe the picture.

1.

- He has a fish in his mouth.
- He and his bike are in the water.
-

2.

**Lesson 20
Day 5**

Describing Things

A. Look at the picture below. First, add two **descriptive** details to describe the picture. (Hint: How many kids are on the swing, and how many kids are there in total?) Next, use all three details to write a sentence to describe the picture.

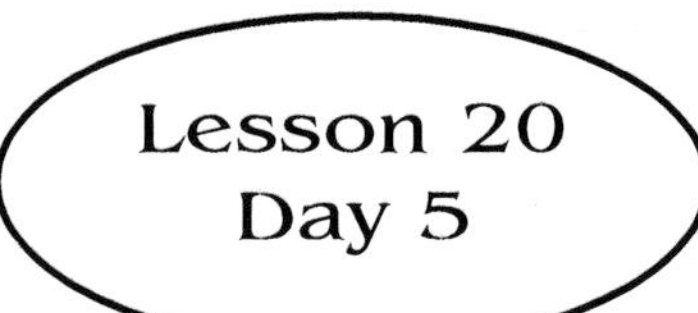

1.

   • The old tire is a great swing.

   •

   •

2.

Describing How We Feel

We have learned that we can use **descriptive words** to describe almost anything. We can even use them to describe how we feel. Words such as happy, sad, glad, mad, excited, sick, healthy, weak, strong, scared, surprised, confused, dizzy, full, hungry, and bored are examples of **descriptive words** we can use to describe how we feel.

A. Look at the pictures below. Use one of the words from the box to describe the way the person in each picture **feels**.

| sick | happy | tired | sad |

1.____________________________

2.____________________________

3.____________________________

4.____________________________

Date:________________

Describing How We Feel

A. Look at the pictures below. Use one of the words in the box to describe the way the object in each picture **feels**.

dizzy   bored   scared   full

1._______________

2._______________

3._______________

4._______________

Describing How We Feel

A. Read each sentence below and underline the words that tell how the person **feels** in each sentence.

1. Dan felt sick and dizzy after the ride.

2. Becky was happy when the baby walked.

3. Shane was mad when he lost the game.

4. Dad was tired after he lifted the rock.

5. The doctor said Troy was healthy.

6. Amy was confused because of the math problem.

7. Kristin was bored with staying inside.

Date:_______________________

Describing How We Feel

A. Read each sentence below. Write a word on each line that tells how you **feel** after each sentence.

____

- -

1. If you eat too much food, you feel ___________________________.

____

- -

2. If you spin around too fast, you feel ___________________________.

____

- -

3. If someone startles you, you feel ___________________________.

____

- -

4. If you have a fever, you feel ___________________________.

____

- -

5. If you have nothing to do, you feel ___________________________.

____

- -

6. If you don't sleep, you feel ___________________________.

____

- -

7. If you do well in school, you feel ___________________________.

Date:___________________

Describing How We Feel

A. Write a sentence to tell how each person feels in these pictures.

1.

2.

Date:_______________________

Describing What We See

In Lesson 21 we learned to write about how we feel. In this lesson we will learn how to write about what we **see**. What words come to mind when you think about things you see? When you see a **car**, do you **see** just a large **thing** that takes you where you want to go, or do you see something that is made from many different parts that each have different shapes, functions (how something works), colors, and textures? When you look at the parts that are combined to make something else, you can use the unique characteristics of those parts to provide more detail in your sentences.

What do you **see** when you look at the **kitchen** in your house? You can look at the kitchen as simply a room where you can eat, sit, or get a drink, or you can look at a kitchen as a place that has painted walls, a stove, small appliances, a table, chairs, and a floor. If you think about it, almost everything you see can be broken down into separate parts.

A. Look at each picture below. What do you see? Write an **X** on the line next to each detail that could be used to describe the detail of **what you see** in each picture.

1. a. ____ The fish is leaping out of the water.

    b. ____ There are three people in the boat.

    c. ____ The boat has sunk.

    d. ____ The boy has caught the fish on his line.

    e. ____ The fish has its mouth open.

2. a. ____ There is a bear riding the bike.

    b. ____ The bear is standing on its head.

    c. ____ There is a bird on the bear's shoulders.

    d. ____ The bike has a front light.

    e. ____ The bike has two tires.

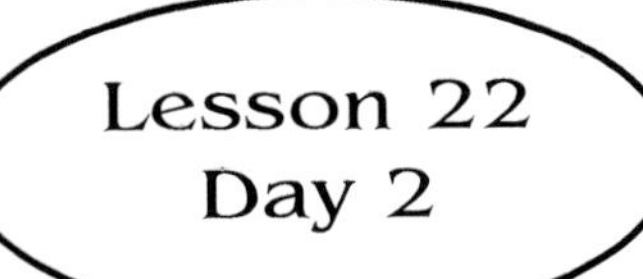

Describing What We See

A. Two details have been added to describe each picture below. Add another detail on the lines to describe each picture. What do you **see**?

1. The clown has striped pants.
   The clown is scared.

2. The horse is bucking.
   The cowboy is falling from the horse.

Date:______________________

Describing What We See

A. Take a look at your **bedroom**. Make a list below of three things you see there. Make sure that these things can be used to provide greater detail about your **bedroom** if you were describing it to someone who has never seen it.

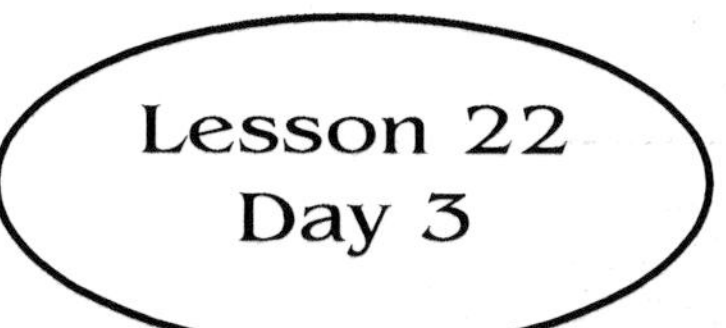

1.

2.

3.

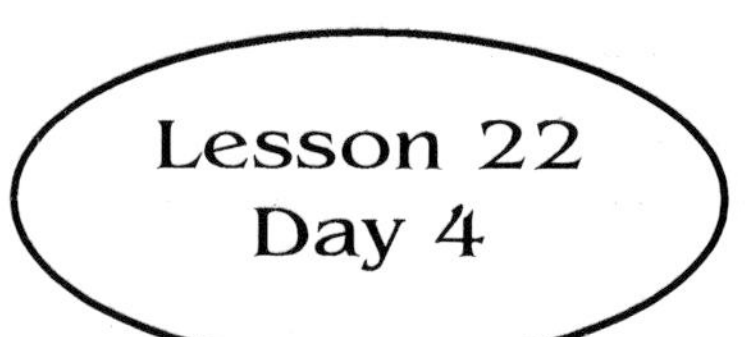

Date:_______________________

Describing What We See

A. Take a look at the **kitchen** in your house. Make a list below of three things you see in your **kitchen** that can be used to provide greater detail about it if you were describing it to someone who has never seen it.

1.

2.

3.

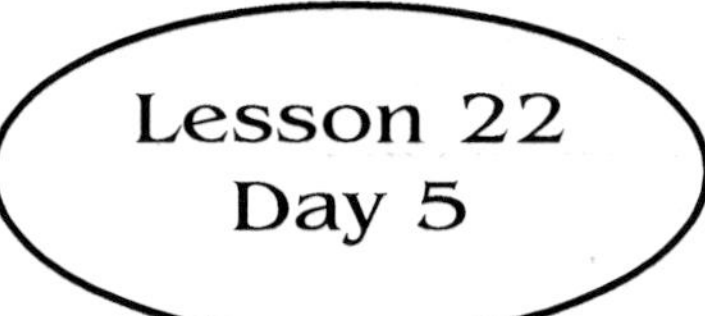

Date:_______________________

Describing What We See

A. Write a short sentence for each picture below that provides more detail than the general description next to each picture. Each sentence has been started for you.

1. **guitar player**

I see....

____

____

____

2. **airplane**

I see…

____

____

____

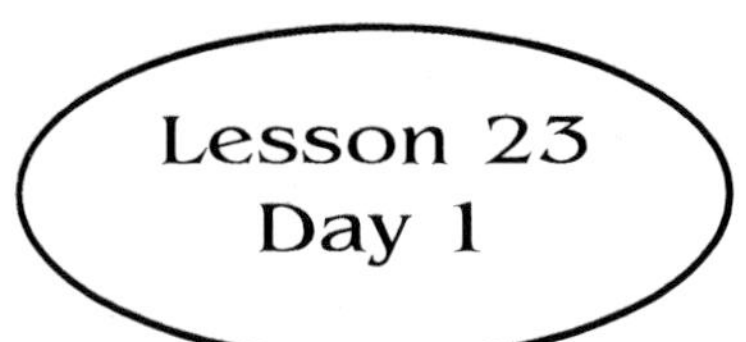

Date:______________

Describing What We Hear

In this lesson we will learn how to write about what we **hear**. What kinds of words come to mind when you think about sounds we **hear**?

If you hear a **glass** fall to the floor and shatter, the sound might be **loud**. If you are listening to a symphony, the sounds might be **soothing** or **relaxing**. **Descriptive words** are used to provide the reader with a much clearer mental picture of what is heard.

For example, read the following sentence.

The cup fell to the floor.

Compare the last sentence to this sentence.

The cup fell to the floor and made a **loud** sound.

You can see that by adding the word **loud** to the sentence, the reader has a much clearer image of what kind of sound was **heard**.

Here are some more examples of how **descriptive words** are used to describe sounds. The **descriptive words** have been underlined.

- the <u>loud</u> roar of the lion
- Mom's <u>soft</u> voice
- the <u>quiet</u> click of the light switch
- the <u>clanging</u> ring of the bell

A. Underline the **descriptive words** in the following sentences that describe sounds you **hear**.

1. We heard the ringing sound of the dinner bell.

2. They heard the booming beat of the drum.

3. The door made a clanking sound as it closed.

4. The popcorn made a popping noise in the pan.

5. The baby let out a loud cry.

6. The crashing thunder woke us.

7. The man let out a shrieking yell.

8. My room is a quiet place.

9. The blaring sound of the siren scared me.

10. The boy spoke in a quiet voice.

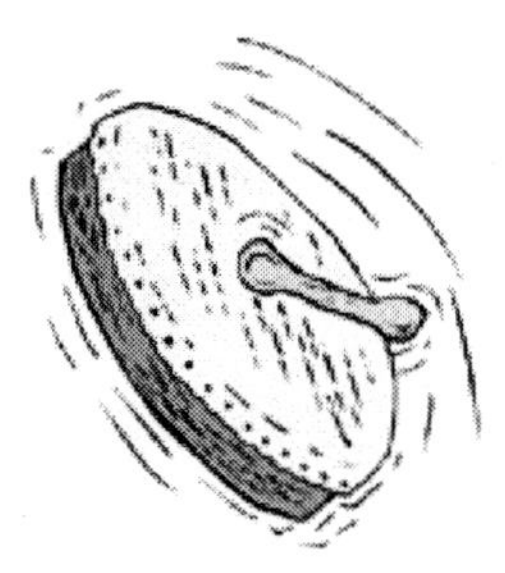

Date:_______________

Describing What We Hear

A. Underline the **descriptive words** in the following sentences that describe sounds you **hear**.

1. The crackling ice was too thin.

2. The thumping horses were coming.

3. The dinging doorbell was pressed.

4. The beeping horn was funny.

5. Tommy let out a loud yell.

6. He spilled the fizzing soda.

7. The splashing ocean was soothing.

8. The squealing pig ran away.

9. The squeaky door woke me.

10. The purring cat was happy.

11. Quacking ducks are fun to watch.

12. Mooing cows are in the field.

13. Howling wolves are scary.

14. The smashing hammer hit the nail.

15. The yelping dog was startled.

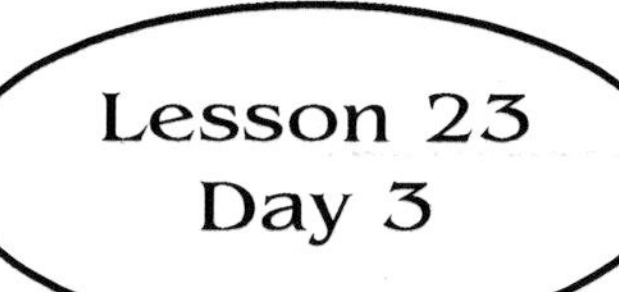

Date:___________________

Describing What We Hear

A. Finish the following sentences with words that describe **sound**. Use the words in the box to complete the sentences below. Remember to use correct capitalization.

ringing	buzzing	quiet
loud	crashing	growling

1. The _________________________ music filled the air.

2. The _________________________ wind was relaxing.

3. The _________________________ cymbal rang out.

4. The _________________________ bell was loud.

5. _________________________ bees are fun to watch.

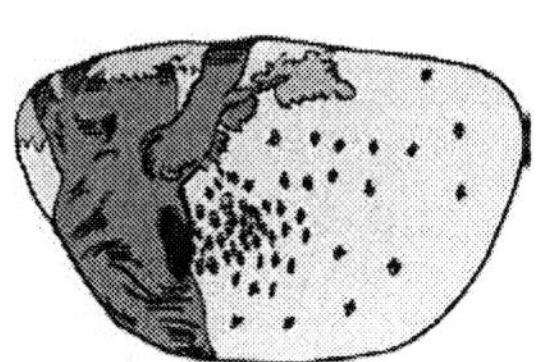

6. The _________________________ bear was angry.

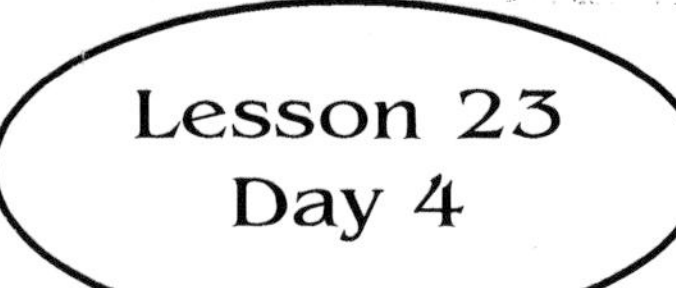

Date:_______________________

Describing What We Hear

A. Finish the following sentences with words that describe **sound**. Use your own words to fill in the blanks below. Remember to use **descriptive words** that describe a **sound**.

1. The _________________________ cows were hungry.

2. The _________________________ wind was loud.

3. The _________________________ cat is his.

4. The _________________________ man is my boss.

5. My _________________________ clock was working correctly.

6. The _________________________ water kept me awake.

7. The _________________________ girl was sad.

Date:____________________

Describing What We Hear

A. For each picture below, write a short sentence that describes the **sound** you would hear.

1.

2.

Review of Grouping
Same and Different

A. Assume we are writing a story about **types of food**. Look at the list below. Write an **X** on the line next to the details that would be appropriate to include in this story.

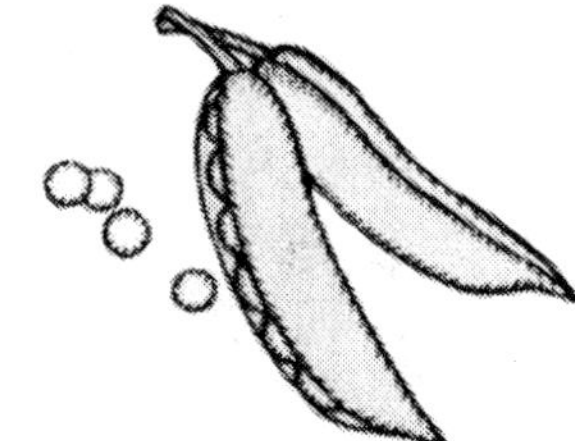

1. ____ spaghetti

2. ____ celery

3. ____ tomato

4. ____ fork

5. ____ macaroni

6. ____ napkin

7. ____ peas

B. Assume we are writing a story about **types of furniture**. Look at the list below. Write an **X** on the line next to the details that would be appropriate to include in this story.

1. ____ couch

2. ____ chair

3. ____ stool

4. ____ front door

5. ____ bed

6. ____ table

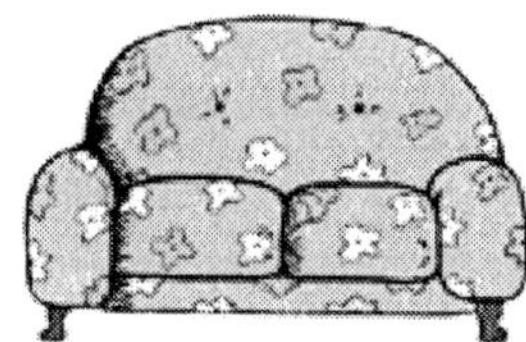

7. ____ chimney

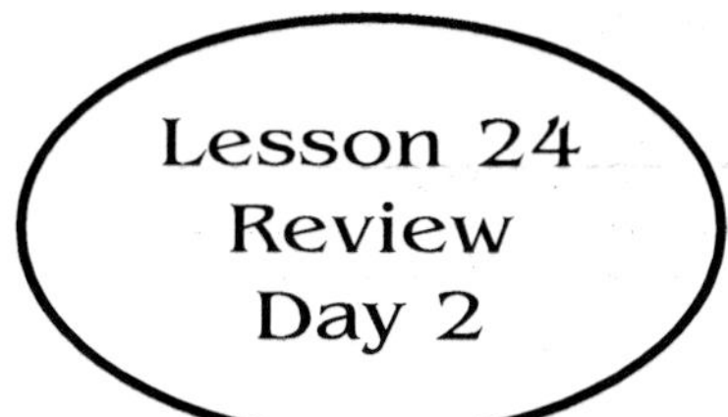

Date:___________________

Review of Describing Things

A. Look at the below picture. You will find below three details that describe the picture. Write your own sentence using all or parts of the three details to describe the picture.

- The robot has a toolbox.
- The robot holds a tool in his hand.
- The robot has a square head.

1.____

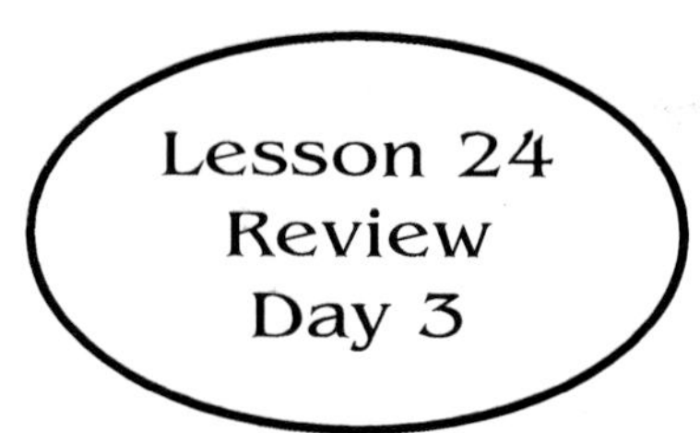

Review of Describing
How We Feel

A. Look at the pictures below. Use one of the words in the box to describe the
way the object in each picture **feels**.

| mad   happy   scared   tired |

1.______________________

2.______________________

3.______________________

4.______________________

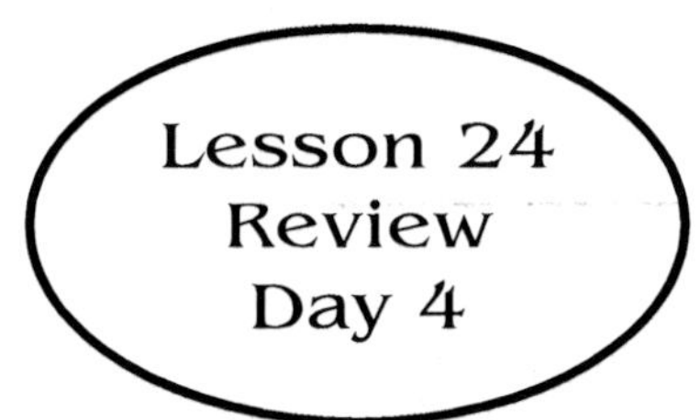

Date:_______________________

Review of Describing What We See

A. Look at the pictures below. What do you see? Write an **X** on the line next to each detail that could be used to describe what you **see** in each picture.

1. a. ___ Two people are juggling together.

   b. ___ Both people are wearing the same costume.

   c. ___ There is a pin dropped on the floor.

   d. ___ The pins have stripes.

   e. ___ They are juggling six pins.

2. a. ___ There are two riders on the bobsled.

   b. ___ The bobsled has the number five on it.

   c. ___ One rider is pointing with his finger.

   d. ___ Neither rider is holding onto the bobsled.

   e. ___ One rider is shouting.

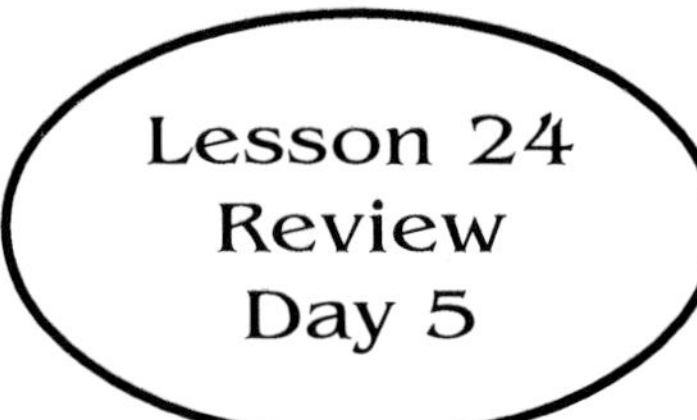

Date:_______________________

Review of Describing What We Hear

A. Finish the following sentences with words that describe **sound**. Use the words from the box to complete each sentence below.

popping	barking	loud
quiet	chirping	ringing

1. The _________________________________ room was a good place to sleep.

2. The _____________________________ thunder woke me up.

3. The ___________________________________ cork didn't fly far.

4. The __________________________________ bird was pretty.

5. A _________________________________ bell was on the boat.

6. The ______________________________ dog was at our door.

Date:______________________

Writing a Title for a Story

A **title** is a group of words that tells or describes what a story is about. Although we covered **topics** in Lesson 13, a topic is not always the title to the story. The topic is often a bit broader than the actual title to the story. Assume that you are writing a story about **girl's shoes**. A very appropriate **topic** might be **girl's shoes**. This is a nice, broad topic for thinking of ideas for your story; however, it might not be a very **interesting** title for your story. A better title might be "**My Funny Sister and Her Shoes**."

The **first** and **last** words of a **title** are always **capitalized** as well as **important words** in the middle of the title. For now, words that should <u>not</u> be capitalized in a title are **the**, **that**, **a**, **an**, **are**, **at**, **by**, **for**, **in**, and **to** (unless they begin or end the title). There is no **punctuation** after a title unless it is written at the end of a sentence.

A. Assume you are going to write a story about the pictures below. Select the best **title** by writing an <u>**X**</u> on the line next to the title you have chosen.

1. 

   a. ___ Making Sandcastles

   b. ___ A Fun Day at the Beach

   c. ___ Playing in the Ocean

2. 

   a. ___ Men Playing Chess

   b. ___ Men Walking

   c. ___ Men Playing Darts

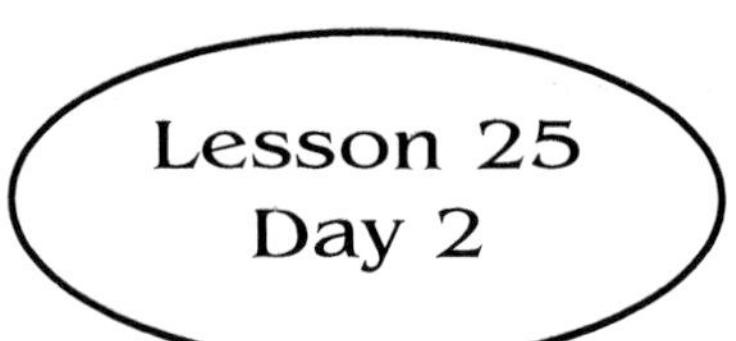

Date:_______________________

Writing a Title for a Story

A. Assume you are going to write a story about the pictures below. Select the best **title** by writing an **X** on the line next to the title you have chosen.

1.

a. ____ The Dolphins Sleep

b. ____ Dolphins Doing Tricks

c. ____ Fish of the Ocean

4.

a. ____ Sounds of the City

b. ____ Man Singing a Song

c. ____ Dan Plays Jazz

2.

a. ____ Bird of Prey Hunting

b. ____ Birds in Flight

c. ____ Wings of Birds

5.

a. ____ Fireman Ready

b. ____ Man Holding Hose

c. ____ Men Wearing Hats

3.

a. ____ Green Vegetables

b. ____ Tomatoes

c. ____ Things to Eat that are Red

6.

a. ____ Things that Bite

b. ____ Cobra on the Loose

c. ____ Reptiles

Date:________________________

Writing a Title for a Story

A. Read the **titles** below and write an **X** on the lines next to the **titles** that are written correctly. Remember the rules from Day 1.

1. ____ The Magical Flute

2. ____ The man and his Dog

3. ____ Swinging in the Tree.

4. ____ My New Car

5. ____ Our Favorite Food

6. ____ The Puppy and his toy

7. ____ The King and I

8. ____ Playing at the pool

9. ____ Going on Vacation

10. ____ The Piano Player.

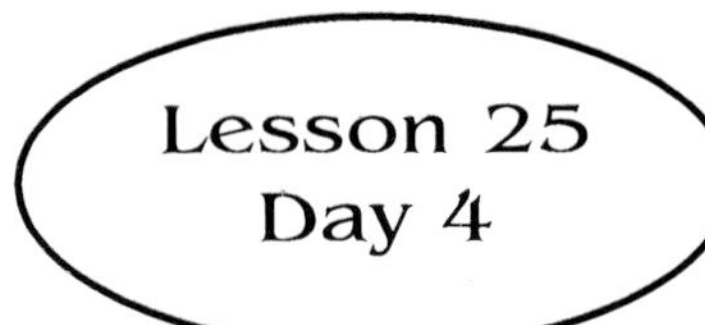

Writing a Title for a Story

A. Read each group of sentences below that tell a story. On the lines provided, write a **title** for each story.

1. It gets hot in the summer.

    Sometimes we go the beach.

    We also play at home in the sprinkler.

    We often go to our neighborhood swimming pool.

Title:______________________________________

2. My family likes to travel.

    Sometimes we go to Grandma's house.

    We often ride roller coasters at the amusement park.

    Sometimes we like to go to New York City.

Title:______________________________________

Writing a Title for a Story

A. Below are the **titles** to two stories. Write three short details (not necessarily full sentences) that could go into each story.

1. My Favorite Toys

a. ____

b. ____

c. ____

2. My Shoes

a. ____

b. ____

c. ____

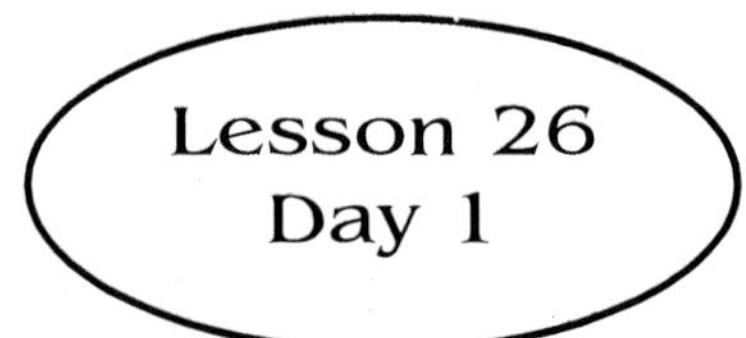

What is a Story

Date:______________________

A **story** is a group of sentences that are related to a common **topic**. Usually the story will also have a **title** which can be the same as the topic, or it can be a more **specific description** of the story (See Lessons 13 and 25).

These related sentences are put together so that there is a **beginning**, **middle**, and **ending** to the story. When a story needs to be told in a certain order, the sentences that make up the **middle** portion begin with the words like **first**, **next**, **then**, and **finally** (See Lesson 15).

A. Below is a **short story**. Underline the **beginning** sentence of the story.

Topic: eating fruit (a general topic for ideas)
Title: "How to Wash Grapes"

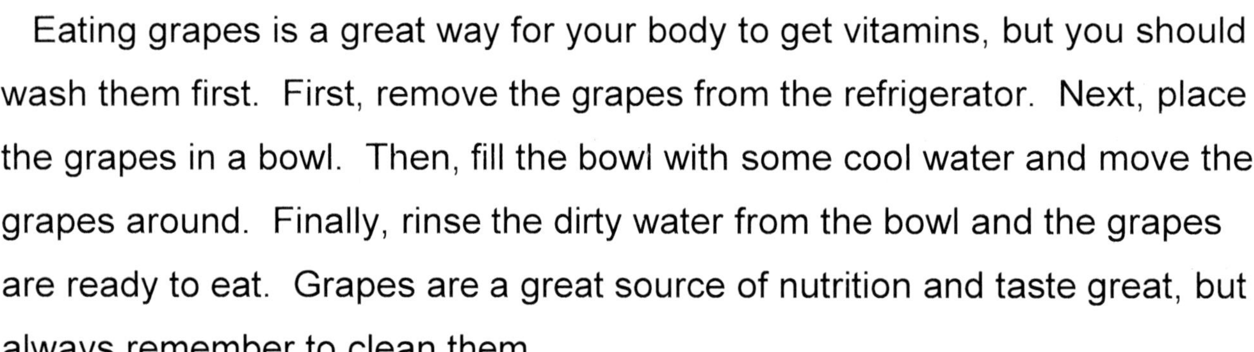

Eating grapes is a great way for your body to get vitamins, but you should wash them first. First, remove the grapes from the refrigerator. Next, place the grapes in a bowl. Then, fill the bowl with some cool water and move the grapes around. Finally, rinse the dirty water from the bowl and the grapes are ready to eat. Grapes are a great source of nutrition and taste great, but always remember to clean them.

B. Below is the same short story as before. This time underline the **middle** portion of the story.

Topic: eating fruit (a general topic for ideas)

Title: "How to Wash Grapes"

    Eating grapes is a great way for your body to get vitamins, but you should wash them first. First, remove the grapes from the refrigerator. Next, place the grapes in a bowl. Then, fill the bowl with some cool water and move the grapes around. Finally, rinse the dirty water from the bowl, and the grapes are ready to eat. Grapes are a great source of nutrition and taste great, but always remember to clean them.

What is a Story

Date:_________________

A. Write a **title** for the story below.

Polar bears are very interesting and fierce animals of the Arctic. Polar bears are large and appear to be calm and peaceful. In fact, polar bears are fierce hunters. Polar bears are very protective of their young and will defend them. Polar bears are meat eaters and will not hesitate to attack at any time. Although polar bears look like they are lovable and calm, they are actually very dangerous animals.

1. ____

B. Does the above story need to happen in a certain order? Circle the correct answer below.

1. **Yes** or **No**

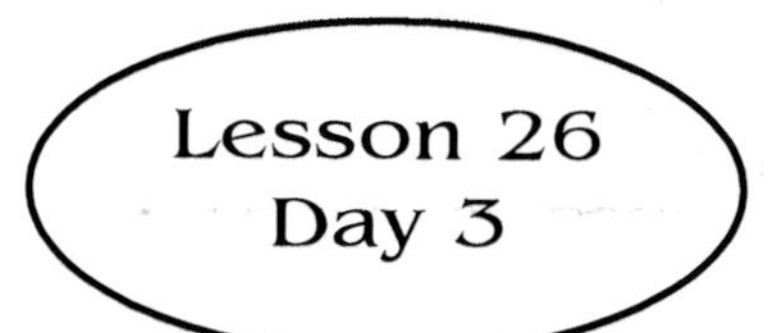

What is a Story

A. Finish the **ending** sentence for the story below.

A baby chicken is fun to watch as it hatches. First, the chick starts by pecking a small hole in the egg. Next, it keeps pecking until it can stick its head out of the shell. Then it wiggles and shakes until it is able to get one of its legs out of the shell. Finally, the fluffy chick is free and can walk around. Watching a chicken hatch is fun because.....

1. _______________________________________

B. Does the above story need to happen in a **certain order**? Circle the correct answer below.

1. **Yes** or **No**

What is a Story

A. Write a **title** for the story of the hatching chicken.

A baby chicken is fun to watch as it hatches. First, the chick starts by pecking a small hole in the egg. Next, it keeps pecking until it can stick its head out of the shell. Then it wiggles and shakes until it is able to get one of its legs out of the shell. Finally, the fluffy chick is free and can walk around. Watching a chicken hatch is fun because it works so hard to get out of the shell.

1. ____

B. Underline the **beginning** sentence of the above story.

A baby chicken is fun to watch as it hatches. First, the chick starts by pecking a small hole in the egg. Next, it keeps pecking until it can stick its head out of the shell. Then it wiggles and shakes until it is able to get one of its legs out of the shell. Finally, the fluffy chick is free and can walk around. Watching a chicken hatch is fun because it works so hard to get out of the shell.

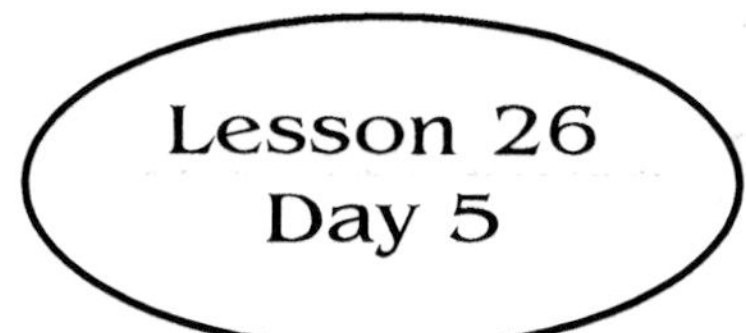

What is a Story

A. Below is a story about **painting a wall in your bedroom**. On the lines below, write a sentence that would fit well into the **middle** part of the story.

I want to paint a wall in my bedroom a bright color. Mom bought some bright paint and a brush. She said she would help me paint. I opened the can without her help, and I carefully dipped the brush into the can.

I got paint all over the carpet, and Mom was not happy. Next time I will wait for Mom to help me when I paint my room.

Date:_______________

Giving Directions

Have you ever had anyone ask you for directions to get somewhere? This is called **asking for directions**. What kinds of words would you use to give directions? Usually we use **words of direction** such as **turn**, **up**, **down**, **left**, **right**, **forward**, **backward**, **curve**, **next to**, **straight**, **ahead**, **U-turn**, **below**, **above**, **north**, **south**, **east**, **west**, **stop**, and **go**.

You will also want to use **landmarks** and **words of distance** to provide clear directions. A **landmark** can be something like a **building**, a **sign**, or some other **easily recognizable object** that the traveler can use as a reference point. For now, we will limit **words of distance** to **feet** and **miles**.

A. Assume that a friend of yours has asked you for **directions** to the **local movie theater**. What two pieces of **information** do you need to know before you can provide him with **directions**? Underline the two pieces of information needed.

1. From where will he begin his journey to the theater?

2. Does he have enough money to get into the movie?

3. Which movie theater does he wish to visit?

4. Who is driving?

B. If you were to receive the following **directions**, where would you arrive?

-Stand up.

-Take three steps straight ahead.

-Turn to the right and take three more steps ahead.

-Once again, turn right and take three more steps.

-Turn right again and take three more steps.

-Sit down.

Look at the choices below. Circle the one that describes where you arrived.

1. in the next room

2. where you started

3. outside

4. somewhere different from where you started

Giving Directions

Sometimes **words of direction** are used in the traffic signs we see when we travel on streets.

A. Write on the lines below to identify the **traffic signs**. Use the words in the box.

right	u-turn	left	stop

1._________________________

2._________________________

3._________________________

4._________________________

Giving Directions

Not only is it important to use **words of direction** and **words of distance** in your **directions**, but also it is important to arrange your **directions** in **order**. If you give directions out of order, the traveler will never arrive at his destination. Remember, the words we use when a story needs to be told in a **certain order** are words like **first**, **next**, **then**, and **finally**. Here is a sample set of directions for how to get to the movie theater:

-First, travel down Oak Street for two miles.

-Next, turn right and travel straight ahead for one mile.

-Then, turn left and travel 500 feet.

-Then, turn right and travel 100 feet.

-Finally, turn left into the parking lot of the movie theater.

A. Number the directions below in the correct order.

1. ____   Next, turn right at Main Street.

2. ____   First, turn left at the stop sign and travel for one mile.

3. ____   Finally, arrive at your destination.

4. ____   Then, travel for five miles on Main Street until you arrive at 3rd Street.

Date:_______________

Giving Directions

A. Can you tell what is wrong with the following two sets of **directions**?
Underline the correct answer in each group.

1. -First, start on 1st Street and travel north for one mile.

   -Finally, turn right on Bacon Street.

   -Next, turn right on 3rd Street and arrive at your destination.

   -Then, turn left on 4th Street and go straight for two miles.

   a. Bacon Street is not a real street.

   b. The directions do not use words of direction.

   c. The directions are out of order.

   d. The directions do not tell where to start.

2. -First, start on 1st Street and travel until you see the water tower.

   -Next, turn left at the water tower and travel for two miles.

   -Then, when you see the red barn, turn right and travel for one mile.

   -Finally, when you see the green car, turn left and travel on Buttercup
   Court for one mile until you reach your destination.

   a. The directions do not use landmarks.

   b. The directions are out of order.

   c. The directions do not use words of distance.

   d. The directions do not tell which way (north, south, east, or west) to
   travel on 1st Street.

Date:_______________________

Giving Directions

A. Think of somewhere in your house other than where you are sitting. Starting from where you are now, give **directions** to this other place in your house. Remember to use **words of direction** and **landmarks** (if necessary). Do not worry about using words of distance. When you are done writing your **directions**, give them to someone in your family for testing to see if they work.

First, ____.

____

____

Next, ____

____

____

Then,

Finally

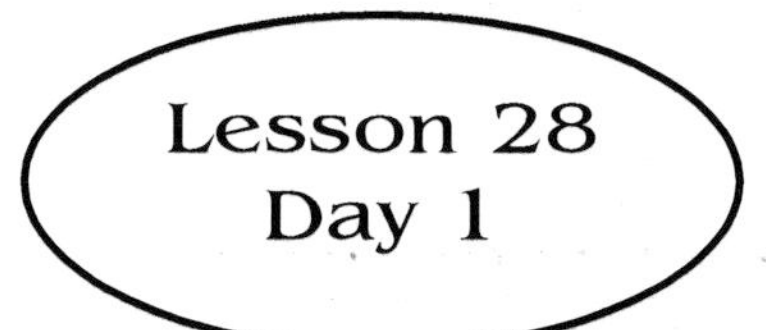

Writing a Story

Date:_______________

In this lesson we will use many of the things we have learned in previous lessons to write a story. What do we need to write an interesting story?

- a topic/title
- a beginning sentence, a middle portion, and an ending sentence
- interesting sentences
- put our sentences in the correct order if we are writing a story about events that must occur in a certain order

Let's start at the beginning and create a **story**.

Just as with any good story, we will need to start our story by first thinking of a good **topic**. We will use this topic to focus our thoughts on related details that we can put in our **story**.

We have selected the topic of **my new puppy**. Now that we have picked a **topic**, we can think of some related details for our **story**.

Thinking about this **topic** for a while, we came up with the following details:

1. My puppy likes to lick faces.
2. My puppy needs to be potty trained.
3. My puppy cries when she cannot sleep in my bed.
4. I bought my puppy a new collar.
5. I had to buy my puppy some special puppy food.
6. I had to take my puppy to the doctor for her shots.
7. I am training her how to go for a walk on a leash.

All we did to come up with details for our topic was to think of things that happened when we first purchased our **puppy**. The problem with these details is that although they are related to the topic (**my new puppy**), they are not **all** related to each other. This makes writing a **short story** rather difficult. Can you see how **taking your puppy to the doctor** is not really related to **buying a new collar for your puppy**?

For our story, let's pick three of the details that are somewhat related to each other.

1. My puppy needs to be potty trained.
2. I bought my puppy a new collar.
3. I am training her how to go for a walk on a leash.

All of these details are related to each other because they are all related to training a puppy. Now that we have selected a few details for our story, we can now narrow our **topic** into a **title**. Our title will be "**Training My New Puppy.**"

A. Now that we have a **title** for our story, underline the sentence below that would make the best **beginning** sentence for our story.

1. My puppy is a good sleeping partner.
2. My puppy barks loudly at people walking outside.
3. My puppy is a lot of fun, but she needs some training.
4. My puppy loves me and licks my face.

Date:__________________

Writing a Story

Here is what we have so far for our story from Day 1.

Title: "Training My New Puppy"

Beginning Sentence: My puppy is a lot of fun, but she needs some training.

Now that we have started our story, let's work on the **middle** part.

On Day 1 we selected the following **details** for our middle part:

1. My puppy needs to be potty trained.
2. I bought my puppy a new collar.
3. I am training her how to go for a walk on a leash.

Is it necessary to place these details in any order? No, this story is not the type that would have to occur in a certain order.

We can fit these details together to form the **middle** part of our story.

> I bought my puppy a new collar and taught her to come to me when I call. I always make sure I have a leash attached to her collar when I take her outside to go to the bathroom. I also use the leash to teach her to stay beside me when we go for a walk.

Notice that we did not use the details exactly as they appeared in our list. Instead, we simply used them as ideas to create sentences for our story.

A. Underline the sentence below that could be used in the story.

1. I also bought a puppy bed that sits beside my bed.
2. I have also taught my puppy to sit when she is on the leash.
3. The doctor said my puppy is healthy.

Writing a Story

We are getting close to finishing our **story**. This is how the story looks so far.

Title: "Training My New Puppy"

My puppy is a lot of fun, but she needs some training. I bought my puppy a new collar and taught her to come to me when I call. I always make sure I have a leash hooked to her collar when I take her outside to go to the bathroom. I also use the leash to teach her to stay beside me when we go for a walk.

The last thing needed to finish our story is an **ending sentence**. A good ending sentence must be related to the rest of the story. It must also either provider a conclusion or it should summarize what has already been said in the story.

A. Underline the sentence below that would make the best **ending** to our story.

1. Going to the doctor with my puppy is not much fun.
2. My puppy is learning a lot and will be fully trained soon.
3. Sometimes I let her sleep with me if Mom agrees.
4. My puppy likes to play with other dogs.

Writing a Story

A. Now it's your turn to write a **story**. Think of a **topic**. Write your **topic** on the line below.

B. Write down five **details** that are related to your **topic**. From these five details underline three that are the most related to each other.

Writing a Story

Assemble your story by using the title, beginning sentence, detail sentences, and ending sentence.

First, think of a **beginning sentence** that will explain to readers what your **story** is about.

Next, think of a good **ending sentence** that either provides a conclusion or summarizes what has already been said in your story.

Finally, write your **story** on the lines below. Remember to use correct **capitalization** and **punctuation**.

Title:_______________

Date:________________

Write About Your Day

In this lesson you will write **about your day**. Did you do anything special or fun today?   Make a list of six **details** that you did today and write them on the lines below. Remember to use **descriptive words** to describe **where you went**, **what you saw**, **what you heard**, **what you tasted**, and **what you felt**.

1.____

____

2.____

____

3.____

____

4.

5.

6.

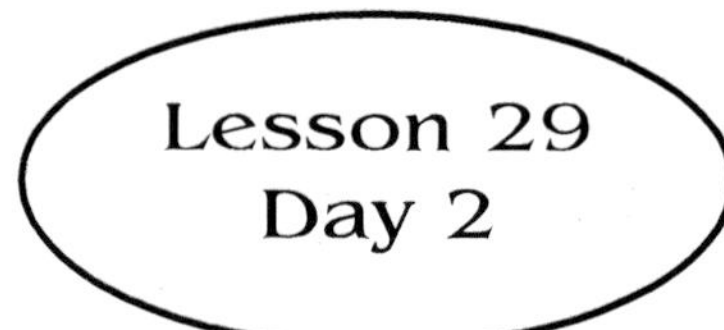

Date:_______________________

Write About Your Day

We know that on Day 1 you started thinking of ideas for a story about **what I did today**. We can assume that the **topic** for the story is something like **what I did today**.

Go back and review your list of **details** from Day 1. Are there any that get your attention more than the others? If three or four of your details are related to going to the zoo, for example, then perhaps the title for your story would be **"My Fun Time at the Zoo"** or something similar.

A. Write your **title** on the lines below.

1.____

B. Select three of your six **details** and turn them into sentences for your **story**. Remember, you do not have to write your sentences exactly like you did your **details** on Day 1. The **details** are only to be used as **ideas** for the sentences in the **middle** portion of your story.

Does your story have to be written in a **specific order**? If so, do not forget to arrange your sentences in the correct order. Write your sentences on the lines below.

1.

2.

3.

Date:____________________

Write About Your Day

A. Now that you have a **title** and three **sentences** for the **middle** portion of your **story** about your day, think of a good **beginning sentence** that tells the reader what the **story** will be about.

It is very important to use **descriptive words** in this sentence since it will be the first sentence a reader sees. This sentence needs to be interesting enough that it makes the reader want to read the rest of your story.

1.

Date:_______________

Write About Your Day

A. You now have a **title**, a **beginning** sentence, and sentences for the **middle** portion of your story (arranged in order if necessary) about your day.

The last part of your story is the **ending sentence**. An ending sentence provides a conclusion or summarizes what has already been said in your story. Write your **ending sentence** below.

1. ____

____

____

____

You have now finished writing your **story**. We will not ask you to rewrite your entire story, but if you were to put the sentences you wrote on Days 1 – 4 in this lesson together, then you would have a complete **story**.

Date:____________________

Write About Your Day

A. Circle the portion of a story below that is the **last sentence**.

   1. the beginning sentence

   2. the middle portion

   3. the ending sentence

   4. the title of a story

B. Circle the portion of a story below that would be arranged in a specific sequence if the story needs to be told in a **certain order**.

   1. the beginning sentence

   2. the middle portion

   3. the ending sentence

   4. the title of the story

C. Circle the portion of a story that tells what the story will be about.

   1. the beginning sentence

   2. the middle portion

   3. the ending sentence

   4. the title of the story

D. Circle the portion of the story that is the **main part** (the largest).

   1. the beginning sentence

   2. the middle portion

   3. the ending sentence

   4. the title of the story

E. Circle the portion of the story that is the final **summary**.

   1. the beginning sentence

   2. the middle portion

   3. the ending sentence

   4. the title of the story

Review of Writing a Title for a Story

A. Read the **titles** below and write an **X** on the lines of the **titles** that are written correctly. Remember the rules from Lesson 25 (Day 1).

1. ____ The Red carpet

2. ____ The Wanderers

3. ____ Eating Lunch at Henry's

4. ____ My old Couch

5. ____ My Favorite Pants.

6. ____ Gardening is easy

7. ____ five easy steps to lawn care

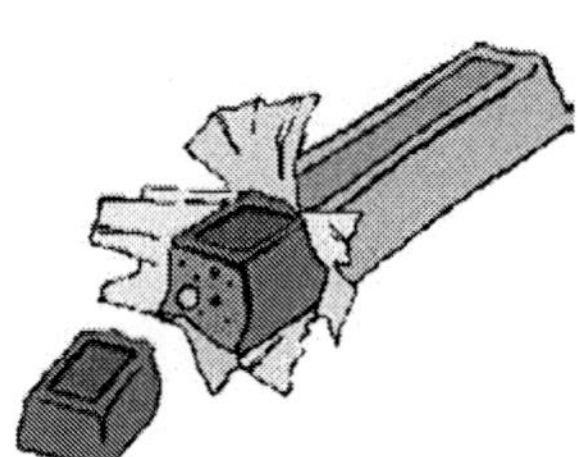

8. ____ Chocolate is The Best.

9. ____ Taking Good Pictures

10.____ The Great Escape

Review of What is a Story

Date:_______________

A. Below is a short **story**. Underline the **middle** portion of the story.

Title: "Types of Poodles"

   Poodles are my favorite breed of dog. They are available in so many different sizes and colors. The largest breed of poodle is the standard poodle. The standard poodle can weigh over fifty pounds. A miniature poodle is the next largest poodle and usually weighs about the same size as a large cat. The toy poodle is the smallest of the breed and usually weighs about the same as a small bag of flour. There are also several different colors of poodles ranging from white to black. Poodles make wonderful pets and are my favorite breed of dog.

B. Underline the **ending** sentence of the story.

Title: "Types of Poodles"

   Poodles are my favorite breed of dog. They are available in so many different sizes and colors. The largest breed of poodle is the standard poodle. The standard poodle can weigh over fifty pounds. A miniature poodle is the next largest poodle and usually weighs about the same size as a large cat. The toy poodle is the smallest of the breed and usually weighs about the same as a small bag of flour. There are also several different colors of poodles ranging from white to black. Poodles make wonderful pets and are my favorite breed of dog.

Date:_______________________

Review of Giving Directions

A. Number the **directions** below in the correct order.

1. ____ Next, turn right after the bank onto Grove Avenue.

2. ____ First, travel south for one mile until you see the bank.

3. ____ Finally, arrive at your destination.

4. ____ Then, turn left on 4th Street.

B. Number the **directions** below in the correct order.

1. ____ First, turn left on Main Street.

2. ____ Next, turn right on Locust Street.

3. ____ Then, drive for three miles on Locust Street.

4. ____ Finally, turn left on Harris Street.

C. Number the **directions** below in the correct order.

1. ____ Next, turn right after the huge rock onto Elm Street.

2. ____ First, travel forward until you see the huge rock.

3. ____ Then, turn left at the old green barn.

4. ____ Finally, travel north until you arrive at the zoo.

Date:_______________

Review of Writing a Story

A. Answer these questions.

1. What is a **detail**? Circle the correct answer.

   a. A detail is the last sentence of a story.

   b. A detail is a group of words that is an idea for a topic.

   c. A detail is the beginning sentence of a story.

   d. A detail is found in the middle part of story.

2. What is a **beginning sentence**? Circle the correct answer.

   a. A beginning sentence starts the story.

   b. A beginning sentence ends the story.

   c. A beginning sentence tells the story.

   d. A beginning sentence is the same thing as the title.

3. Which part actually **tells the story**? Circle the correct answer.

   a. the beginning sentence

   b. the title

   c. the ending sentence

   d. the middle part of a story

4. Which part **summarizes** the story? Circle the correct answer.

   a. the beginning sentence

   b. the title

   c. the ending sentence

   d. the middle part of a story

Date:______________________

Review of Writing About Your Day

A. Make a list of six things you did today. Write them on the lines below. Remember to use **descriptive words** (adjectives) to describe **where you went**, **what you saw**, **what you heard**, **what you tasted**, and **what you felt**.

1.

2.

3.

4.

5.

6.

The Friendly Letter

A **friendly letter** is one that you write to someone you know. It usually **shares information** that is more personal or **asks for information** that is more personal than you would find in a letter sent for business reasons. A **friendly letter** has **five** parts. They are the **heading**, **greeting**, **body**, **closing**, and **signature**.

Let's start at the beginning and explain each part.

Heading

The first part of a friendly letter is the **heading**. The **heading** is in the upper **right corner** of your letter and contains the **writer's address** and the **date**.

Example: 123 Main Street
Prairie, IN 46001
March 3, 2006

Remember to place a **comma** between the **city** and **state**. Also, a **comma** belongs between the **date** and the **year**.

Greeting

The second part of a friendly letter is the **greeting**. The **greeting** usually starts with the word **Dear** followed by the person's name. The greeting is followed by a **comma**.

Example: **Dear** Uncle Ralph,

A. Write an <u>X</u> next to the **heading** that is written correctly.

1. _____ 100 Main Street   3. _____ 100 Main Street
            Hopedale IL 61747   Hopedale, IL 61747
            October 2, 2000   October 2, 2000

2. _____100 main street   4. _____ 100 Main Street
            Hopedale, IL, 61747   Hopedale, IL 61747
            October 2, 2000   October 2 2000

B. Write an <u>X</u> next to each **greeting** that is written correctly.

1. ______ Dear Ted,   3. ______ Dear lee,

2. ______ dear mark   4. ______ Dear David,

C. Write this **heading** correctly. Remember to use **capital letters** and
    punctuation where needed.

800 Salt avenue
tremont IL 61568
june 23 2000

The Friendly Letter

On Day 1 of this lesson we learned about the **heading** and the **greeting** of a **friendly letter**. In this part of the lesson we will learn about the remaining three parts, which are the **body**, **closing**, and **signature**.

Body

The **body** is the third part a **friendly letter**. The **body** includes the message you want to write. Each paragraph should be **indented** half an inch from the left margin of the paper.

Example: I just got my report card and I am excited to tell

you that I received all good grades. Hopefully I can do it again

next semester. I can't wait to see you and Grandpa

next week.

Closing

The **closing** is the fourth part of a **friendly letter** and is the way we say goodbye. Typically, the **closing** in a friendly letter uses words like **Yours truly, With love, Your friend,** or something similar after the **body of the letter**. The first word of the **closing** is capitalized and a **comma** is placed after the **closing**.

Example: Yours truly,

Signature

The **signature** is the fifth and last part of a friendly letter. This is simply the name of the letter writer. The **signature** is placed directly below the **closing**. The **signature** can be handwritten or typed. Below is an example of the closing and signature as they are written together.

Example: Yours truly,
Carlene

A. Write an <u>X</u> next to each **closing** that is written correctly.

1. ______ Sincerely,   3. ______ In Kindness,

2. ______ Your, friend   4. ______ Your cousin,

B. Write an <u>X</u> next to each **closing/signature** that is written correctly.

1. ______ Sincerely,   3. ______ Alex,
          anne   Sincerely

2. ______ Your friend,   4. ______ Your cousin,
          Jacob   Kristin

The Friendly Letter

A. Write the letter on the correct line below for each part of this **friendly letter**.

| **A**=greeting | **B**=body | **C**=signature | **D**=heading | **E**=closing |

1.______

2.______

3.______

4.______

5.______

100 Main Street
Los Angeles, CA 96061
June 1, 2000

Dear Grandma,

    I am very excited to visit you next month. Will Grandpa take me fishing again? I cannot wait to bake cookies with you. Danny says to tell you hello and that he also looks forward to our visit.

Love always,
Tina

The Friendly Letter

A. Write an **X** on the line for each correct answer.

1. Which part of a **friendly letter** tells from where the letter is being sent?

    a. ___ heading

    b. ___ greeting

    c. ___ body

    d. ___ closing

    e. ___ signature

2. Which part of a **friendly letter** tells **from whom** the letter is **written**?

    a. ___ heading

    b. ___ greeting

    c. ___ body

    d. ___ closing

    e. ___ signature

3. Which part of a **friendly letter** is the **main part**?

    a. ___ heading

    b. ___ greeting

    c. ___ body

    d. ___ closing

    e. ___ signature

4. Which part of a **friendly letter** says **goodbye**?

    a. ___ heading

    b. ___ greeting

    c. ___ body

    d. ___ closing

    e. ___ signature

The Friendly Letter

Date:____________________

When your **friendly letter** is finished you will need to mail it. Before the letter is mailed you will need to properly address an **envelope**.

An envelope has **two** addresses. The **first** is the address of the person **sending** the letter. This is written in the **upper left-hand** corner and is called the **return address**.

The **second** address is of the person **receiving** the letter. This is written in the **center** of the envelope and is called the **mailing address**.

Example:

Lee Smith
100 Main Street
Denver CO 80201

        John Peterson
        500 East 5th Street
        Pittsburgh PA 15207

The United States Postal Service suggests not using commas or periods when addressing an **envelope**.

Finally, place a **stamp** in the upper **right-hand** corner. Your letter is now ready to be mailed.

A. Write an <u>X</u> next to the **envelope** that is written correctly.

1. ______

> Jenny Green
> 500 Camp Street
> Orlando FL 32804
>
> Janine Jones
> Pittsburgh PA 15207

2. ______

> Jenny Green
> 500 Camp Street
> Orlando FL 32804
>
> Janine Jones
> 500 South Third Street
> Pittsburgh PA 15207

B. Address this **envelope**. Write the **sender's address** in the top left. Write the **receiver's address** in the center.

Sender's Address	**Receiver's Address**
Darrin White	Brian Smith
950 Pine Street	700 Hemlock Drive
Austin TX 78703	Ames IA 50010

The Thank You Note

A **thank you note** is a quick message that you write to someone to thank them for doing something for you. A thank you note is very similar to a friendly letter except that it does not have a formal heading portion. Instead, a **thank you note** has the following sections: **date**, **greeting**, **body**, **closing**, and **signature**.

Let's start at the beginning and explain each part.

Date

The first part of a thank you note is the **date** which is located in the upper right corner of your note. You will notice that unlike a friendly letter that contains the sender's address as well as the date, the thank you note only contains the **date** portion.

Example: March 11, 2011

Remember to place a **comma** between the **date** and the **year**.

Greeting

The second part of a thank you note is the **greeting**. The **greeting** usually starts with the word **Dear** followed by the person's name. The greeting is followed by a **comma**.

Example: **Dear** Uncle Ralph**,**

A. Write an **X** next to the **date** that is written correctly.

1. ____ October 2 2000   3. ____ October 2, 2000

2. ____ october 2, 2000   4. ____ October, 2, 2000

B. Write an **X** next to each **greeting** that is written correctly.

1. ____ dear Ted,   3. ____ Dear Lee,

2. ____ Dear Mark.   4. ____ Dear David,

C. Write this **date** correctly. Remember to use **capital letters** and **punctuation** where needed.

may 16 2011

The Thank You Note

In Day 1 of this lesson we learned about the **date** and the **greeting** of a **thank you note**. In this part of the lesson we will learn about the remaining three parts, which are the **body**, **closing**, and **signature**.

Body

The **body** is the third part a thank you note. The **body** includes the message you want to tell the recipient. A **thank you note** is usually only a few sentences in length. The body of the **thank you note** lists the good thing the recipient did and why you are thankful for this good deed. When the thank you note is written because someone gave you a gift, it usually includes a sentence or two about why you like the gift and how you will enjoy the gift.

Example: I want to thank you for the gift I received for my birthday. I love puzzles and look forward to putting this one together with my family. We will spend a lot of fun time putting it together. I will send you a picture of it when it's done. Thanks again and I can't wait to see you soon.

Usually **thank you notes** are written close in time from the date when the kind deed was performed. It is typical for a thank you note to be written within 30 days from the kind act.

<u>**Closing**</u>

The **closing** is the fourth part of a thank you note and is the way we say goodbye. Typically, the **closing** in a thank you note uses words like **Yours truly, With love, Your friend,** or something similar after the body of the note. The first word of the **closing** is capitalized and a comma is placed after the closing.

      Example: Yours truly,

<u>**Signature**</u>

The **signature** is the fifth and last part of a thank you note. This is simply the name of the person who wrote the note. The **signature** is placed directly below the **closing**. The **signature** can be handwritten or typed. Below is an example of the **closing** and **signature** as they are written together.

      Example: Yours truly,
                           Carlene

A. Write an <u>**X**</u> next to each **closing** that is written correctly.

1. ______ Best regards,   3. ______ Your Friend,

2. ______ Thinking of you,   4. ______ Your uncle.

B. Write an <u>**X**</u> next to each **closing/signature** that is written correctly.

1. ______ Sincerely,   3. ______ Tim,
             Kim   Sincerely

2. ______ Your cousin,   4. ______ Your friend,
             Ann   Jacob

Lesson 32
Day 3

Date:________________

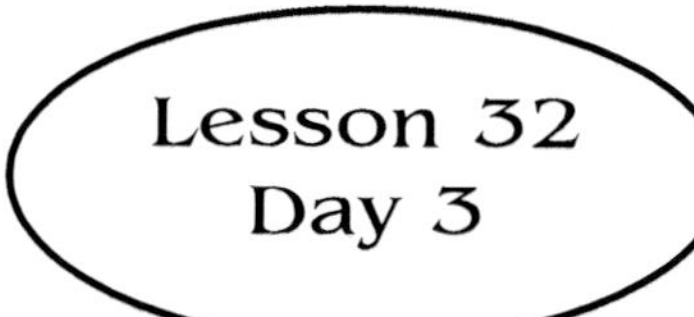

The Thank You Note

A. Write the letter on the correct line below for each part of this **friendly letter**.

A=greeting	**B**=body	**C**=signature	**D**=date	**E**=closing

1. ______

June 1, 2000

2. ______

Dear Grandma,

3. ______

Thank you so much for the new sweater. It is starting to get cold here and I look forward to wearing it soon. It is so pretty and colorful. I will wear it next time I visit. Thanks again.

4. ______

Love always,

5. ______

Kris

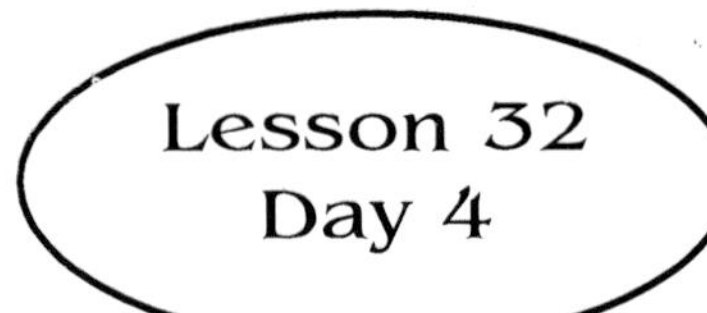

Date:_______________________

The Thank You Note

In this exercise you will write a short **thank you note** to someone for giving something to you or doing something nice for you. Think back to the last couple of days when someone did something nice for you. Write them a quick **thank you note**. For now, we will concentrate only on the **greeting** and the **body** portions of the thank you note.

Dear _______________________________,

Date:______________________

The Thank You Note

A. Correct the following parts of a **thank you note** and rewrite them below.

1. december 18, 2000 (date)

____

- -

____

2. Your Friend,   (closing)

____

- -

____

3. Dear cathy,   (greeting)

____

- -

____

4. Which part of a **thank you note** contains the message portion?

a. ____ date

b. ____ greeting

c. ____ body

d. ____ closing

e. ____ signature

Comparing Things

In this lesson we will learn about **comparing things**. When we compare things we are trying to determine if things are the **same** or if they are **different**.

How do we know if something is the **same** or **different** from something else? It depends on what we are comparing. Are we comparing their appearance (size, color, or shape), the sounds they make, how they taste, or how they function? Opinions on whether or not things are the **same** or **different** can vary among people.

Here is a picture of some tomatoes and grapes. Are they the same or different?

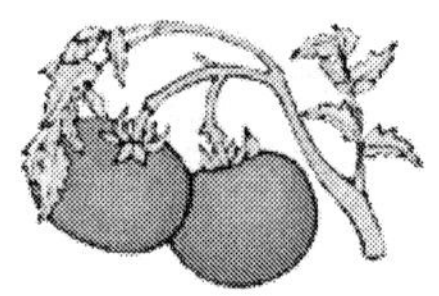

It depends on what features we are comparing. If we are only trying to determine if both are some type of **food**, then they are the same. If we are comparing the **shapes** of the food, then most people would probably say that they are the same (a grape and a tomato are both round). On the other hand, if we are comparing the **size** of the food, most people would probably say that they are not the same (a tomato is usually much larger than a grape). If we were comparing the **taste** of the tomato and the grapes, most people would say that they taste very different.

A. Answer the below questions. Circle the correct answer.

1. Are these pictures the same shape?   (**Yes**   or   **No**)

2. Are the **pictures** below of these items the same size? (**Yes**   or   **No**)

3. Are the pictures below both types of food?   (**Yes**   or   **No**)

4. Do the apple and tomato taste the same?   (**Yes**   or   **No**)

Comparing Things

Date:_______________

A. Look at the items below. Does each pair perform the **same** function? In other words, do they accomplish the same tasks? Write **yes** or **no** on each line.

1. _______________  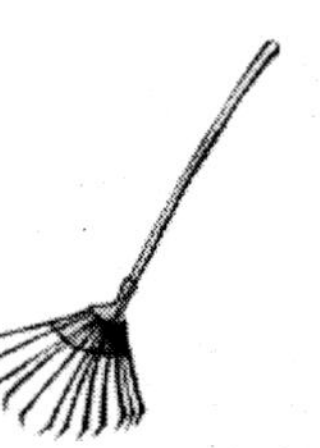

2. _______________  

3. _______________  

4. _______________ 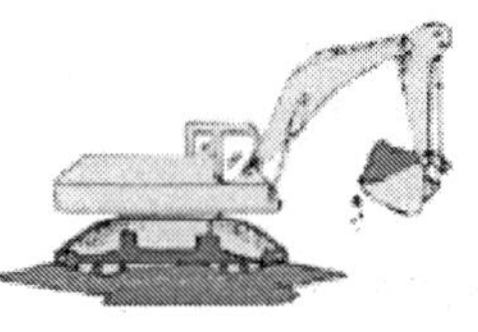 

5. _______________  

6. _______________  

Comparing Things

Date:________________

A. Match the objects that are similar in some way by drawing lines to connect them.

1. football

2. bell

3. hamburger

4. water hose

5. grill

6. pencil

a. french fries

b. fire hose

c. oven

d. bell

e. pen

f. soccer ball

Date:______________________

Comparing Things

A. Circle the items in each group that are similar in some way.

1.
 a.   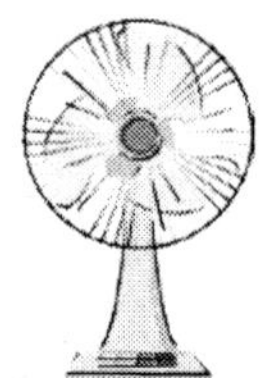 b.   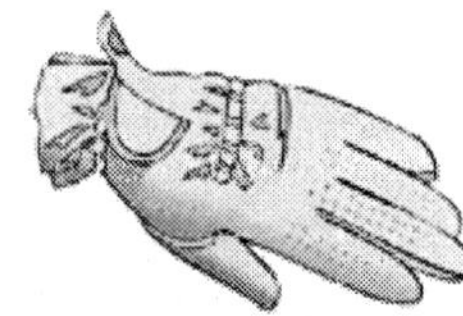 c.

2.
 a.    b.    c.

3.
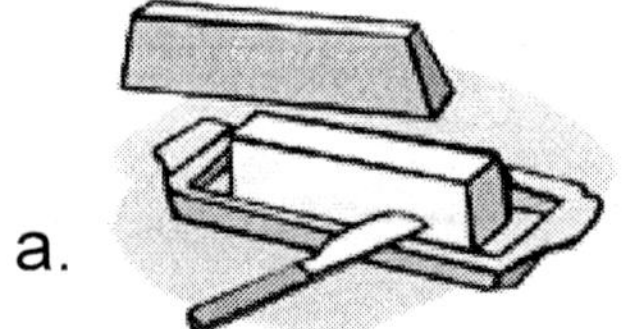 a.    b.   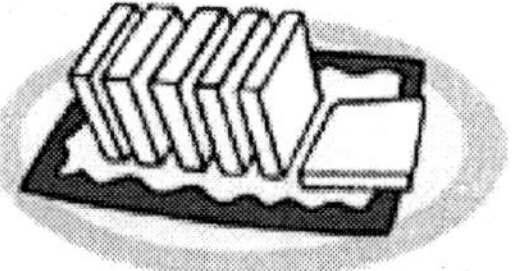 c.

4.
 a.    b.    c.

5.
 a.    b.    c.

6.
 a.    b.    c.

Date:_______________

Comparing Things

A. Look at each pair of pictures.   Write on the lines below **how** they are the **same**. Write the words **size**, **shape**, **function**, or **taste** on the lines to describe how they are the same. There will be more than one word for each pair.

1.

2.

Riddles

Date:________________

A **riddle** is a **statement**, **question**, or **phrase** that asks the reader to solve a puzzle or answer a tricky question. Look at these fun riddles.

What does a lady bug use to keep her hair in place? *bug spray*

How was the earthworm able to afford a house? *he got it dirt cheap*

A. Answer the following riddles by underlining the correct answer.

1. What did one bee say to the other?

   a. Go away!

   b. Buzz off!

   c. Beat it!

   d. My how time flies.

2. Why do spiders make good baseball players?

   a. because they climb up walls

   b. because they spin webs

   c. because they can catch flies

   d. because they are good at batting

3. What do you call an 800-pound gorilla?

   a. anything he wants you to call him, politely

   b. big monkey boy

   c. Mr. Furry back

   d. an overgrown monkey

4. What month has 28 days?

   a. February

   b. December

   c. March

   d. All of them

Date:____________________

Riddles

A. Answer the following **riddles**. These are just for fun. Don't worry if you can't figure them out.

1. What kind of gum do bumble bees chew?

2. How do you tell a bug to go away?

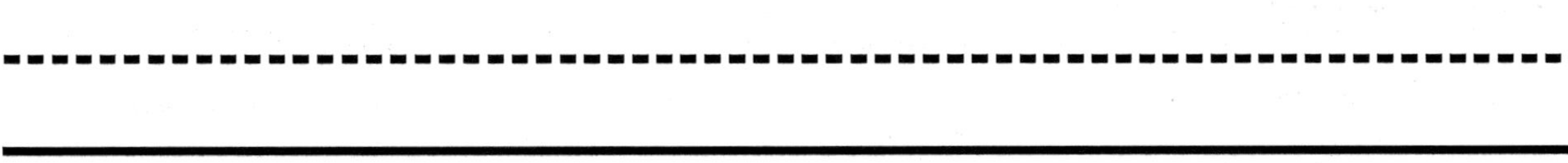

3. What happens when a fly hits a baseball?

4. Do fleas go the mall?

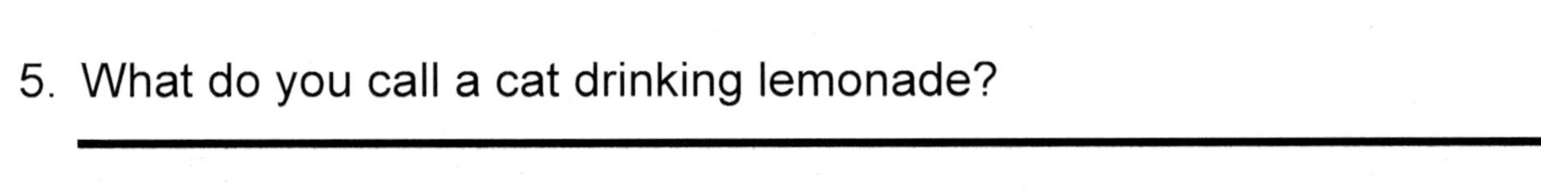

5. What do you call a cat drinking lemonade?

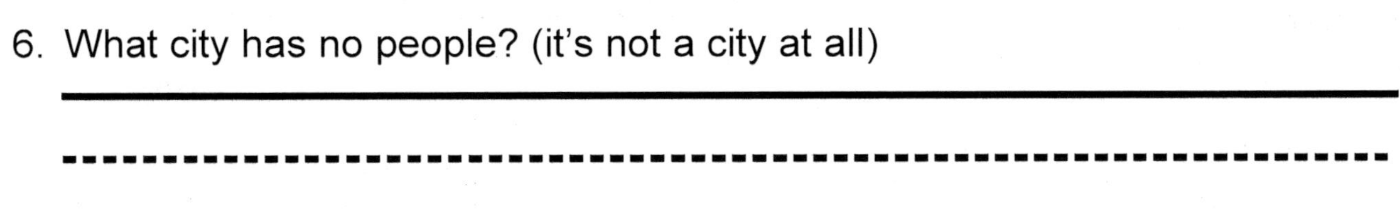

6. What city has no people? (it's not a city at all)

Riddles

Date:___________________

Let's write a **riddle**. We will start by looking for a word that has more than one meaning. For example, the word **bug** has more than one meaning. One meaning of the word **bug** means an **insect**. Another meaning of the word **bug** means **to bother someone**.

A. Here is a riddle for you to answer. After looking at both definitions for this word, we are able to think of the following riddle:

Why does Anne the ant dislike door-to-door salesmen?

Answer: ____

Riddles

Date:________________

Let's try another riddle. Once again, let's think of a word that has more than one meaning. For example, the word **hit** has more than one meaning. One meaning of the word **hit** is **to strike something**. Another meaning of the word **hit** is a **music recording that is very popular**. With that in mind, write an answer to a riddle that includes the word **hit**.

A. Here is a riddle for you to answer.

What happened when the boxer recorded a music album?

Answer: _______________________________________

Riddles

Date:_______________

This time try to write a **riddle** on your own. You can start with a word that has more than one meaning. Here are a couple of words you can choose from, or you can think of one of your own if you like.

Beat - One meaning of the word **beat** is **to win at something**. Another meaning of the word **beat** is **to strike something**.

Trip - One meaning of the word **trip** is **to fall or stumble**. Another meaning of the word **trip** is **to go on a journey**.

Remember to place a question mark at the end of your **riddle**.

Question:____

Answer: _______________________________

Creative Writing

Creative writing is when we write about something by using our imagination. You can write about anything at all. For example, if you could close your eyes and picture in your mind the **perfect bedroom**, what would it look like? What color would it be? What would it smell like? How big would it be? You can imagine what kind of story you could write just by answering these questions.

A. What colors would you paint your bedroom? Write a sentence to explain.

B. What kinds of things would you want in your bedroom? Perhaps you would
want a carnival ride or a bowling alley. Be creative and write a sentence
about it.

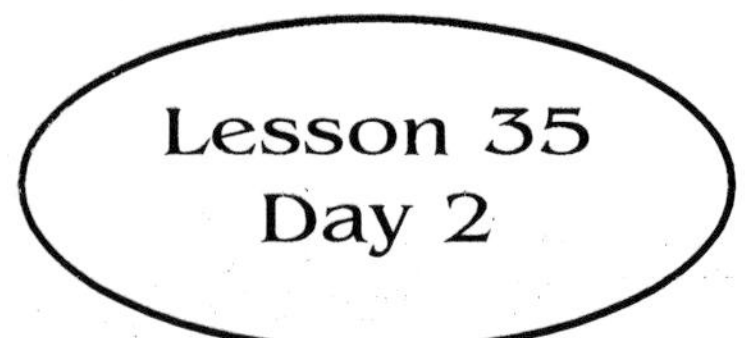

Creative Writing

Let's keep working on your perfect bedroom. You have already written about the color you want it to be and what kinds of neat things you want in it. What else can you do to describe your room? Would your room have any particular smell like cotton candy or pizza? Maybe you could have a machine that makes your room smell like whatever you want. How big do you want your room to be? Should your room be large enough for just you, or should it be big enough to have sleepovers? Maybe it should be as large as a soccer field.

A. What would your room smell like?

B. How large is your perfect bedroom?

Creative Writing

Date:________________

Let's keep working on your perfect bedroom. You have already written about the color you want it to be, what you want it to smell like, what kinds of neat things you want in it, and how large you want it to be. How else can you describe your perfect bedroom? Would you like a drink machine in your bedroom? It could have water, soft drinks, or different kinds of juices in it. Do you want any real or stuffed animals to live in your room? Maybe a parrot or a friendly elephant would be fun.

A. Assume you would like to have a drink machine in your bedroom. What kinds of drinks would it serve?

B. What kinds of animals would you like to have in your bedroom? If you do not
want any animals in your bedroom, think of something else you would like to
have.

Date:_______________

Creative Writing

We are almost done with your perfect bedroom. Have you given any thought to what type of furniture you want in your room? Would you want bunk beds or perhaps a huge bed the size of a basketball court? Do you want a television in your room or perhaps many televisions? If so, how large and how many televisions do you want?

A. What kind of bed do you want in your bedroom?

B. What kind and how many televisions do you want in your bedroom?

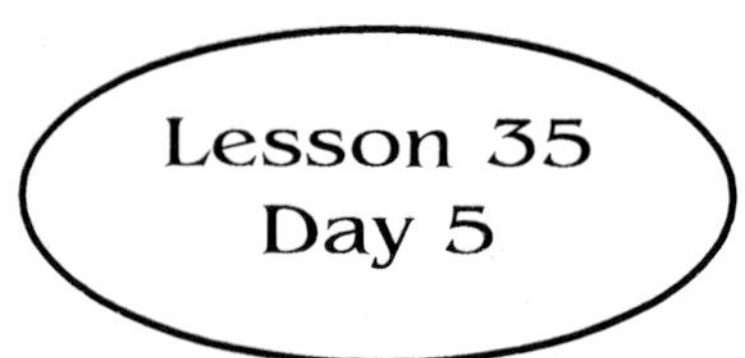

Creative Writing

Go back and look at the sentences you wrote on Days 1 through 4 of this lesson. Choose three sentences from the group. Write the three sentences you selected below. Hopefully you wrote interesting sentences with lots of **descriptive words**. If you didn't write interesting sentences, add some descriptive words as you write them on the lines below. Are there any other ways to make your sentences better?

Once you get the three sentences the way you want them, write a story on the lines below about your **perfect bedroom**. Remember to use an **introductory sentence**, a **middle** part (use your three sentences here), and an **ending** sentence.

Remember to use correct **capitalization** and **punctuation**. A **title** for your story is already provided for you below.

Title: **My Perfect Bedroom**

Date:_______________________

Review of the Friendly Letter

A. Write an **X** next to the **heading** that is written correctly.

1. _____ 500 South Street
Atlanta, GA 30341
January 1, 2000

3. _____ 500 South Street
Atlanta, GA 30341
January 1 2000

2. _____ 500 South Street
Atlanta, ga 30341
January 1, 2000

4. _____ 500 South Street
Atlanta, Georgia, 30341
January 1, 2000

B. Write an **X** next to each **greeting** that is written correctly.

1. _____ Dear, Mike,

3. _____ Dear Lee,

2. _____ dear mark

4. _____ Dear David,

C. Write an **X** next to each **closing** that is written correctly.

1. _____ Thanks,

3. _____ With Kindness,

2. _____ take care,

4. _____ Yours kindly,

D. Write an **X** next to the **closing/signature** that is written correctly.

1. _____ Sincerely,
janet

3. _____ Alex,
Sincerely

2. _____ Bob,
Thanks

4. _____ Your friend,
Kristin

Level 2, Lesson 36 - Review of Lessons 31-35

Review of the Thank You Note

A. Correct the following parts of a **thank you note** and rewrite them below.

1. April 8 2000 (date)

____

- -

____

2. thanks, (closing)

____

- -

____

3. Dear Grandma (greeting)

____

- -

____

4. Which part of a **thank you note** is the main part?

a. ____ date

b. ____ greeting

c. ____ body

d. ____ closing

e. ____ signature

Review of Comparing Things

Date:________________

A. Answer the below questions. Circle the correct answer.

1. Do these items taste the same?   (**Yes** or **No**)

2. Are these items the same size?   (**Yes** or **No**)

3. Are the pictures below both types of food?   (**Yes** or **No**)

4. Do the pencil and the marker do the same kind of thing? (**Yes** or **No**)

 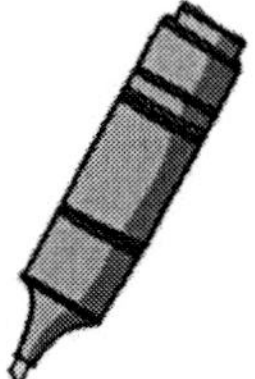

Review of Riddles

Date:______________________

A. Answer the following **riddles** by underlining the correct answer.

1. Why did the woman wear a helmet at the dinner table?

    a. in case the chandelier fell

    b. in case a food fight happened

    c. she was on a crash diet

    d. she was just getting ready to ride her scooter

2. Why are teddy bears never hungry?

    a. because they sleep during the winter months

    b. because they just ate a few hours ago

    c. because their mouths are sewn shut

    d. because they are already stuffed

3. Why was the belt arrested?

    a. because it was too tight and hurting its owner

    b. for holding up the pants

    c. because it couldn't behave

    d. because it could not get along with its buckle

4. What did one potato chip say to the other?

    a. nothing, a chip cannot talk

    b. something salty

    c. would you like to go for a dip

    d. hi, my name is Chip

Date:_______________

Review of Creative Writing

Think if you could build a **toy** that looks the way you want or does whatever you want.   Write three sentences below and describe what this toy would look like or what it would be able to do.   Use **descriptive words** and **strong verbs** to make your sentences interesting.

Once you get the three sentences the way you want them, write a story on the lines below about your **toy**. Remember to use an **introductory sentence**, a **middle** part (use your three sentences here), and an **ending** sentence. Remember to use correct **capitalization** and **punctuation**. A title for your story is already provided for you below.

Title: **My Super Toy**